The Itinerate Circus

New and Selected Poems 1995-2020

∾

George Looney

The new poems in this collection originally appeared in the following journals:

The Journal: "Slow Dance with Hummingbirds in Erie"
Alaska Quarterly Review: "Stories Told in Inconstant Light"
The Greensboro Review: "Tonight the Moon's Made of Whale Song"
The Missouri Review: "Riffs Thelonious Put Down" and "An Occurrence of Grace at a Bartok Concert" (These two poems were part of a group of poems which won the 2003 Larry Levis Editors' Prize in Poetry from *The Missouri Review.)*
Prairie Schooner: "A Country Song Where the Moon's Lost"
Willow Springs: "Gene Study Shows Whales Are Close Relatives of Hippos"
Xavier Review: "Months of Close Work with Ice"
Witness: "Animals Posed Severe"

Other poems in this collection originally appeared in the following journals:
Alaska Quarterly Review, Alligator Juniper, American Literary Review, Ascent, Bateau, Bayou Magazine, The Bellingham Review, Cimarron Review, Cold Mountain Review, Cottonwood, Denver Quarterly, Flint Hills Review, Flyway Literary Review, Gulf Coast, Hayden's Ferry Review, Janus, The Journal, Kestrel, The Laurel Review, LIT, The Literary Review, Midday Moon, Natural Bridge, New England Review, New Letters, Notre Dame Review, Prairie Schooner, Pudding Magazine, Puerto del Sol, Quarterly West, The Southern Review, The Sow's Ear Poetry Review, Third Coast, The Tule Review, and *Whiskey Island Magazine,* and in *PP/FF: An Anthology.*

ISBN   978-1-952204-00-5

Printed in the United States of America

RED MOUNTAIN PRESS

Seattle, Washington

www.redmountainpress.us

For poetry makes nothing happen: it survives
In the valley of its making

—W.H. Auden

Dear Lord,
we lurch from metaphor to metaphor,
which is—let it be so—a form of praying.

—Andrew Hudgins

New Poems

from *ANIMALS HOUSED IN THE PLEASURE OF FLESH*

from *ATTENDANT GHOSTS*

from *THE PRECARIOUS RHETORIC OF ANGELS*

from *OPEN BETWEEN US*

In memory of Douglas Smith, gone now
but there through it all

New Poems

It starts with a woman singing her son to sleep
in Wayne, Ohio. In the library,
the homeless recite familiar rosaries of loss

in the stacks. The first snow has dropped
power lines, homes in Wayne dark or candlelit.

Here, the lake doesn't let anything go
and the sky wants to be sung to sleep.

That woman singing in Ohio might be a ghost.
No doubt any of us might haunt
what we call our lives. Everywhere,

placards with faces of the missing blur with weather,
forgetting names behind the senility of weeds.

In Wayne, failed vision has led to cul-de-sacs
and exhaustion. The faithful fumble
through old hymns, the sky gone bitter.

A drunk curses gulls here that curse the lake.
His kids have been missing years,
he swears. No one gives a damn.

Hummingbirds, he used to call them.
His little red-throated ones. In Wayne,

the past is lost enough the dead could starve,
and snow comes down amnesic.

Here, some kids outside sing of doubt and love,
certain no one listens,
their fevered throats carved by hacking.

Wayne's backyard wells often taste of sulfur,
the local dead faded first names on stones
in a cemetery thick with rumors of old corn.

From the word go, music couldn't comfort stones
cut with names or a drunk, stumbling
past closed-up stores, calling for his kids.

11

~

All the sweet water in the world isn't enough,
Champlain. A storm's moved in off Erie,
the sky the memoir of some verbose eclipse,

and loss can't be escaped on planes folded
out of corn husks, no matter the wind.

In Wayne, local produce is rumored
to turn to song on the tongue. Remember

the cursing drunk, his hands almost blurs?
Imagine him home, singing
sugary lullabies, his children never having

gone missing. Imagine those kids outside
stay out and sing despite the storm
and mothers yelling at them to *Come inside.*

Have you lost your senses? You're going to
catch your death. The same story,

despite the weather or place. Music, it's said,
is about time, but saying that's too easy.

Truth is, all this singing wants to blur the faces
on placards so no one's left missing,
and the dead slow dance with children.

In Wayne, a hint of corn and sulfur on her tongue,
a woman kisses her husband's neck.

Here, the storm over, a woman kicks up puddles
and sings a fifties ballad about love and loss,

holding, on her shoulders, her son, who laughs
and says *Mommy* over and over until it's a song.

STORIES TOLD IN INCONSTANT LIGHT

The moon is cavalier
—Richard Hugo

To say those homes went dark different hours
says nothing. Might as well say

a brute lived alone with his rancorous, knuckled god
in the last house of that cul-de-sac.

Dogs flinched at his scent. Or say a pale sliver of
a woman loved him despite it all,

and dogs howled at her sweeping that porch,
dust doing sad acrobatics in decaying orbits.

It's hard to say for sure just what love is.

One night I snuck out late. I swear
there was music in the brute's house

and light inside flung shadows over the grass.
They danced in what I'd have to say was joy.

Every dog that roamed the street lowered
its long head and whined,

meaning this was worth suffering for. The moon
had nothing on the light

those figures flickered in, and no screen
at a failing drive-in

could tell a better story or refurbish
a tired heart and sell it off for a profit

despite run-down shacks to either side.
Who would have thought

the brute had the grace to dance? Not one of us
had the gumption to ask

the pale woman rarely seen out what love was,
though the faint marks on her arms

13

~

the crudest of us named seas
surely were chants in some desperate language,

part of a ritual which left water confused and the heart
with every window open to dry out.

Nights, the inconstant light of the drive-in
across the road calls everything

into question, like that lawn where shadows danced
to a music I was too young to imagine.

That none of us had a clue was years off.
That the brute knew sorrow, even further.

That love makes room for violence is something
no flickers on a screen can explain.

TONIGHT THE MOON'S MADE OF WHALE SONG

The landfill simmers, collapsing
under a finned moon. Sour oysters

stink behind a restaurant whose name
ends with stylized waves.

Say *lover* and the moon dives deep, a dog
howling at four a.m.,

the body you hold just an excuse, nothing to do
with gravity. The tide has

no way to remember or forgive
without the moon, which collapses

into song and the arms of a lover
no constellation could guess the name of.

Water is less and less sure about direction
or what dogs bury for the moon.

When the landfill's covered with sod and fog
it's another world—the moon

a tyrant, dogs howling perfect Portuguese.
For now, perfumed with whiskey

and lemon, the moon collapses of its own weight.
All over town spent lovers simmer

under memory. Faint scars reflect what light
drifts through fractured blinds. Say *moon*

and lovers dream of painting the figures of dogs
on cave walls long before the thought of art.

Say the body you touch is the one
direction you're sure of.

RIFFS THELONIOUS PUT DOWN

The landscape here is flat enough
turkey buzzards circle with nothing dead.
Some howl in my body says *home*,

but memory's a map folded up
wrong, every street a dead end.
Store fronts lit up downtown

could bluff a pair of deuces
to the moon. Over the bar,
sober and fatalistic ghosts dance

to nostalgic riffs Thelonious
lays down. Light at dusk is
a flush, a hand difficult to beat.

The stoic moon holds its face cards,
hoping for a high straight.
It's too pale this early to make anyone fold.

The ghosts of veterans who won't dance
play poker, a heartache
or better to open. Bitter

whiskey reminds me where the bodies are
buried, "Straight, No Chaser"
howling out the jukebox. Tone-deaf

ghosts scrape a piano in need of tuning
over the floor upstairs.
Down the bar, a drunk woman

awkwardly signs blurred sentences,
her once deft hands dancing
these days for rain. Rough weather

has forgotten this town, the sky
mute. A sax has taken up
what Monk and his blunt fingers laid out

on a piano so sober it couldn't bluff
a straight. I'm so much in the hole
no one hand could pull me out,

not even Monk's. This the last dregs
of Ohio, ghosts know
the moon likes to bluff but fold anyway,

the pot too rich. I'm trying to pick up
the deaf woman. Holding
her hands leaves us nothing

to talk about. Buzzards, grotesque
fruit, snore in the trees.
Thelonious is sober, ready to call it

a night. The ghosts don't know
enough to call it quits.
Tickle dem bones, they beg

Monk's shade, and he does. Only
the deaf woman is drinking.
Last call sent everyone else home

with six-packs and regret. Her hands
fumble what could be words
on my hollow chest. The moon

has stumbled off with everyone's pasts,
the ghosts muttering how
it cheats. Whatever Thelonious

might pound out over the bar,
land's too flat here
to hold anything good for long.

The deaf woman lives miles
to the south. The ill-folded map
can't guide me there. Even drunk,

her hands remember touch
used to be another, better language.
The way they move now,

she couldn't pound love from any piano.

A COUNTRY SONG WHERE THE MOON'S LOST

All roads lead to this truck stop, the word *Eat*
doing a number on the dark,

slopping over the road and beckoning to cars
far enough back their headlights aren't a bother,
the landscape flat enough light has no arc to it.

Maybe back under *Eat* they'd say, Take a load off.
Time was the waitresses there would bless

the worst sinner with a kind word, and trucks
carted off regret no scales could hope to measure.

What would they say if I walked to the next weigh station
and stood on the scales and refused to budge

until they measured my sorrow? Nothing for it,
I guess, but to get off at the next exit, turn around

and come back to *Eat* washing over this road,
a tide not ruled by the moon or its contradictions.

Nothing but the touch of a waitress in a truck stop
can hope to measure the hard miles
of a heart driven without sleep too many nights.

The moon's having trouble sticking around.
Every time *Eat* flashes, it's gone.

Not even the constellations and all their lies
will get to me, the air warm with grease, thick
enough to lean on. My arm, where she touched it,

hums a country song where the moon's lost a woman
to a trucker's hard lovin' and hangs in the sky,

~

a sliver of its former self. My heart, waking,
picks up the tune and whistles it. Every vein
leads to the memory of a touch, the music enough

to make up, a little, for what the moon has
lost. The cargo of my heart can't be
weighed by any scale along this road tonight.

GENE STUDY SHOWS WHALES ARE CLOSE RELATIVES OF HIPPOS

Every night I drive through this town,
its name rusted off the one sign
for miles, dust acrobatic in my headlights.

Last night, a drunk stumbled, sobbing, home
I figured, with some inherited sorrow.

Maybe the sorrow the hippo sings, lost
in some foul, drought-shrunk pond or river,

cut off from any ocean with whales, barnacled,
who would understand the song and hum it
across the world. This town is

a question of lineage, the drunk familiar enough
his DNA, left at the scene of a crime,
could convict me. Despite the abandoned church,

its stained-glass saints missing hands or feet or hearts
knocked out by rocks hurled drunk,

faith is sung by people every Sunday in homes
in desperate need of repair. Truth is,

the priest couldn't keep the saints straight
and left town to head north for an ocean
to hunt whale. Not for oil or perfume,

but song. Cathedrals that swim, he called them,
their vast architecture enough to forgive any sin.

He wanted to be swallowed and decades later
have his feeble bones be found
surrounded by those gull-stripped flying buttresses

the wind is a hymn passing through. The church
collapsing in the middle of town has
no window with a hippo behind a miraculous saint,

but a whale does strut in the lead-fractured
portrait of a saint whose heart is open sky.

~

Some hymns, sung drunk, can shatter glass,
stained or not. Water cuts the hardest
of liquor or wind to something palatable,

and the local bar stinks of prayer and songs sung
in some language full of gutturals I can't pronounce.

The way sorrow snorts in a corner, massive, gray and oily,
any saint would choose to give up, pack it in,
and pawn everything for a ticket to points north.

The last house before the anonymity of fields
is empty, its walk feeble with weeds,
its wrecked windows reliable witnesses

to the aim of local kids who won't make it
onto this town's farm team, the mascot
a landlocked rodent without any sort of song.

If they'd trade for me, I would buy the house,
let the town drunks with paunches and no arms

think of it as home, and welcome back an ex-priest
with bones so waterlogged they hum.

But the team doesn't need another pitcher
with a tired arm. The house collapses. Tonight,

the same drunk stumbles home, sure nothing he'd sing
will touch the heart of a saint, much less
shatter it. Across town, too much dust on home,

the visiting pitcher grinds the ball in his glove
while the ump stirs the dust into acrobatics
no one will mention later in the sad excuse for a bar

where both teams will drink under a fiberglass whale
strung on a wire from the ceiling, the heart
in its empty body a pair of old speakers.

Music will come out of those ribs I will dance to,
even with no church to bless or damn the dance,

even if the dance isn't one that could ever produce
enough grace to keep a defrocked priest in
a ruined church, or wave a drunk, safe, home.

AN OCCURRENCE OF GRACE AT A BARTOK CONCERT

This concerto could cripple a sky.
The woman in the wheelchair
wants her voice to be the viola

and, for a moment, it is. Beautiful,
its guttural tone, from
enough distance, could be mistaken

for the rosined scrape of the bow.
What is love for this woman,
her hands demented buzzards

flapping in her lap, her body
a kind of grave
carnival-mirror imitation

of a body? Without enough control
to form words, her mouth
has gone slack, a bitter cavern,

the acoustics no consolation.
Music's impossible
without pain, a dead composer

said alive. If he was right,
this woman's crippled body
could be the most beautiful allegro

ever composed for strings, unplayable,
perfection no one living
can appreciate. No one has heard

the viola in her voice before.
At the beginning
of the last century, she'd have been

dolled up in scales and factory workers,
their drab wives left home,
would have paid pennies to see her

flap around in a shallow pool,
the Fish-Woman.
They'd have heard whales in her voice,

seaweed and rust, not Bartok.
Those vain hawkers of deformities,
who charged men to touch suffering

flesh masqueraded as mystery,
weren't interested in grace.
Their shrill voices are too often ours.

The man who wheels this woman away
from the music, to stop
her voice, has lifted her out of

water, loving how her body clutches itself,
the spine a fist closing,
knuckles white down her twisted back.

Has he come to think love's a freak show,
a necessary complement of
the light bulbs, accordions and laughter

of wavy figures in warped glass?
The itinerate carnival,
without it, drifting between towns,

no one believing its loud insistence
that joy exists? Has he
drawn petroglyphs on her flesh

with his tongue, like those on rocks
in the Southwest, long
dead voices still loving the earth

in translation? Is her body any more
crippled than any one of us
brought to our knees by this concerto?

Is music loss we can bear because
of its beauty? The heart
isn't something we speak of these days.

Nothing consoles us, it turns out.
Still, the most crippled body
is capable of more joy than

any dead composer. And this
music risen, warped, out of
this woman could bring any sky

to its knees. The way buzzards,
in flight, from
a distance, can define grace.

High in the Sangre de Cristos, Bach
    was crystalline tonight,
played on an orchestra of ice ephemeral

as music itself. The conductor
    stumbled home, drunk.
His wife, in some dingy hotel room,

kissed her lover's bald spot
    as he snored.
The two of them, the conductor

and this faithless woman, have
    denied each other
hymns Bach drank to forget.

The violins of ice steamed. Maybe
    the sculptor who carved
the cold, clear orchestra wakes

the morning after with a memory
    of the absolute
precision of Bach and a woman

who kissed his bald spot
    as if she meant to
breathe a music through him

that would keep going long after
    the flesh has left
the bones dreaming of touches

they were always under but
    never felt. Bone
concertos are different than Bach

played on ice. Marrow resonates
    with the warm history
of passion. Ice is the photograph

of water blurred by its turning
    away. To carve wind
and string instruments out of this

is to clarify the loss music is
    born of. The conductor
can't remember his father.

His mother trembles on the floor,
    a torn white slip
clutched in her hands, her knuckles

whiter than snow in the Sangre de Cristos
    in March. He can't
comfort her. Like everything

that belongs to the past,
    she is memory,
and revision, it seems to

the conductor, drunk again,
    is a sin. That
the man who carved an orchestra

of ice caresses the naked
    and frustrated wife
of the conductor in a hotel room

is no accident, but a story
    of longing and distance
acted out by desperate figures

whose lives strand them within
    sad scenes of storms
and crystalline cold. Nothing

recorded last night matters after
    the instruments return
to water. It was, after all, the ice

that mattered, the clear way
    the steaming violins
and oboes and the rest held

the notes. The conductor's wife
    has never held
any lover with such longing.

The ice sculptor, his hands
    losing the cold
from months of close work with ice,

kneads the tense muscles of her back
    and whispers librettos
in her ear. The conductor, drunk

at home, curses the cold front
    moving in and imagines
the local, late night weather woman

has settled, naked, on his lap.
    His raw hands caress
her almost ephemeral back.

Her arms hold him like nothing has.

ANIMALS POSED SEVERE

A verdict comes back after so much
time we had forgotten
the long-sequestered jury. So gray

is our desperation, we prefer
fog to the memory
of color. A carnival has come to town

humming unfamiliar tunes
power lines and street lamps
take up. Children make up lyrics

about carnies and loss they sing to
what has come to be
the town humming. We can't

get a straight answer as to where
the forgotten jury has been,
but they reek of cotton candy

and salted nuts, their faces the ghosts
of carousels, animals
posed with nostrils flared and poles

passed clean through midsections. Guilt
isn't the question. Rules
of evidence go out the window

when a good hawker gets going
with oddities to sell.
Music the horses and the rest dance to

is enough to set anyone free, but
the prizes displayed in booths
aren't worth what they cost

to win. The jury is interviewed,
their biases fodder
for rumors and dry enough

goats and llamas choke and hack up
things that are gray.
We hum songs we loved

28

when we were innocent, experience
having taught us music
has a nasty way of turning

on anyone who thinks it's theirs.
Children turn up missing.
The verdict the jury comes back with

is *guilty*, but they've been out so long
the judge has released
the defendant on his own recognizance.

Several of the jurors suggest
he's taken the children.
The police believe it's carnies,

and get busy tearing up the carnival
looking. Even the animals
posed severe on the carousel are nervous,

the music they circle to different, edgy.
The owner of the carnival
is found asleep by a road, drunk.

The officers who bring him in
leak to the press
the goat found with him, threatening

to bite, had denim on its breath.
A court order to have
the goat put to sleep and cut open

waits on a clerk's desk to be signed.
The judge hasn't come back
from the carnival. He's having

lunch, the children who circle him,
rigid in his robe,
singing nonsense he can't follow

over the wood splintering under axes
the police use to leave
nothing to chance. The llamas

start backing off when children
stick their hands through
chain-link fences to pet them. Too much

going on for trust to make it through.
One of the forgotten jurors
turns up missing. His wife,

hysterical on the local news, pleads
for his return. *No one
will listen to me*, the nervous woman

says, *but him*. The carnival's owner,
alone in jail, prays
all the nonsense about children missing

has nothing to do with him.
Memory, he'd confess to
anyone willing to hear, can return

a verdict we have to appeal.
Fog can be a kindness,
he wants us to believe. Instead,

we believe anything just passing through
can't be trusted. It is
the carnival, we know. That's why

things have come up missing. If this
were another country,
we might take and burn him, singing,

drunk. But this is a country
of laws. Rumor is,
the last meal the missing juror had

was goat, the music in the air Greek
and played by old men
with sour breath, weak with ouzo

and thin blood. *Humor them*, his wife
is reported to have said,
clapping in bad time to feeble music.

Now, her body trembles with a tune
all too familiar. Tragedy
gets high marks for being easy

to dance to. And any music makes
an issue of time. The way
children, missing or circling

a somber man in a robe and singing,
can remind us what has
already been lost, the carousel a moan

under their skin. The instructions
the jury got from the judge
never had a chance. To lead us to guilt,

all it takes is a song that's been on
the juke box as long
as any drunk can remember. Pick it,

and any one of us any night might confess.
The goat's returned to
the carnival, breath free of any hint

of fabric. The word comes down
to strike the tents
and make ready to move on.

The children thought missing
are found playing
in a shack near the motley tents

collapsing in rhythms as calm
as the breath of a drunk,
asleep, the woman touching him

in his dream forgiving him
everything. Fog drifts in
over the hints of men tearing down

any chance of color. The animals are
shrouded and shipped off.
Guilt's what we're left to live with.

from Animals Housed in the Pleasure of Flesh

A trick of light, and the strokes in an etching by Dürer
coalesce into the figure of a woman on a porch
with what could almost be a wolf or coyote
beside her, its wind-stroked fur an etching
of dirty ice on a river scorched by blades.

Surfaces teach us of love. The way a snowfall changes
the longing of the land for whatever sky's been emptied.
The way any surface is the result of distance.
As if it weren't us. As if the world were not
what we make it, pulled by dogs down streets so dark
the sound of a river is almost a kind of light.

In the Dürer, light forms the musculature
of Adam's arm as it reaches for the single leaf
on the body of Eve, a body nearly of light, both
bodies fields where light whispers in the grass
named by the touch of light. And desire
is the sound of what could be a river in the dark.
Having heard the Ohio in a woman you've touched,
you want to listen to rivers you haven't heard.

The woman on the porch could speak of the *Salzach*,
the *salt river*, which could almost convince you it's not
water, but turquoise you could cut stones from
to give to a woman who, on a dare, once balanced
on the rail of a fragile bridge high above the river.
The gulls complained at her being almost of the air.

Pound wanted to gather out of the air a live tradition.
What could be more alive than the river
in a woman? What is the buried tradition of rivers?
In particular, any river of salt which carves
what may be desire in your body, the memory
of a woman who is light, since light names
all bodies of vision, or water, or what it carves.

Dürer's Eve is carved of light. And desire
is what the snake wants to bite into, not the apple,
which is the wrong fruit anyway. Even the fruit
is a lie. Even a dirty river can be turned. Like
the Ohio was turned more than a hundred years ago
by the earth rising along a faultline. Willows

35

on islands in the river twisted and broke, uprooted
by water moving a new way. The dead of
New Madrid, Illinois slid in, moved by confusion.
All rivers carry off both memory and desire,
the dead one form the desire for memory takes.
Those neglected bodies became silt, like a family
dropped by a bridge collapsing into the *Salzach*
that was forgotten in the salt cursing of water.

Inside a house near the river where a woman
drinking coffee almost saw the bridge collapse,
frescoes of baroque devils whisper of the water
in bodies that carves desire like the lines Dürer made
to form the shadows which shape the delicate flesh
of Eve's hand with the apple. It's not clear
whether Eve means to offer the apple to Adam, the snake,
or to the darkness almost moving behind them
which can only be God. The two figures of light
could be standing on the porch of a house with frescoes
painted by a bruised madman laughing on his back.

It could be snowing, the *Salzach* scarred by the blades
of men whose breath rises from bodies warm
with memory. The snow could almost be burning
in a light from the house or whatever moon is left
like longing in the sky whispered
by a woman who's been bruised by flesh
and blood devils in a winter ritual when
the anger that etches the dour bodies of men
is acted out, their faces grotesque masks.

Or it could be summer, the river the Ohio.
Light could touch the surface and be mistaken
for desire, or love, or the nearly-forgotten language
Dürer etched words from in an open book
hung over a branch to claim this Adam, this Eve.
Or the gray light of winter could claim a woman
walking a dog by the Ohio and remembering another river
in a landscape Dürer would know the language of.
Her skin could be the light Dürer wanted to claim for Eve,
or the apple. It would be, if not for how the gray
longing of the Ohio sky seems to bruise her body.

The river is not closed off yet by ice, and you are
no ghost, no dead engraver. You want to name a river
after the distant mountain goat Dürer put in

36

the one place of light in the landscape other than
the bodies of Adam and Eve. You want
to bury your hand in its fur and feel what light can
only imagine, knowing this would be different
from the fur of masks worn by the *Krampusse*,
masks too large to be mistaken for anything human.
In some countries, bruises on women's bodies
in winter could form the goat's name, and fear
is a miracle that pierces the skin of saints. In Ohio,
a woman says what could be a name or its ghost,
her breath rising gray by a half-frozen river.

And desire could be where rivers come together
in a woman, flowing into one another
to form one body both flesh and the memory
of flesh, desire, and the light that's a longing
in the bodies Dürer cut out of darkness
which, left untouched, was only a god.
And no god can reconcile the distance
the river in a woman flows, or name the light
on its water, or the form of longing it cuts.

IN YOUR BASEBALL DREAMS

after Richard Hugo

It starts innocently enough. Grass burns in light you believe
isn't real. At first there's only one man, a soiled glove
slipped over his left hand. Or else there's a man and a woman
in the uncut grass of a field you once read a corpse
was discovered in, the head crushed by what the news said
could have been a baseball bat. The woman's shirt drapes
the man's left hand. The wind covers his fingers in cloth
and strokes a thin gauze of pollen around their bodies,
and yours. The woman turns her naked back to the man,
whose hands pull her jeans into the grass. She's on her knees,
touching the man's scrotum, when you remember this
started with a man, a glove, and a ball coming at you
as if you have to do more than just watch in this dream.
And you do. You catch the ball in the glove you always knew
bandaged your left hand. Dust and pollen explode the air
around your eyes. You sneeze. And the woman is lost
in the grass under the man, her voice lifting like an insect
from the almost yellow wild grass. It hasn't rained in weeks,
her back singed by the brittle blades. Like the ones
cutting into your bare feet as you heave the baseball back
to the man who has turned away from you. Before
you can warn him, another man catches the ball.
The sound it makes collapsing into his glove echoes
the distant curse of a bat connecting with a woman's skull
which opened to let the violence slip into the grass,
and through the grass into the soil which you can taste now
as the baseball hits your glove again. Off in the grass
the man is tasting the woman, his tongue trying to
articulate a force in this woman who has pollen
and stiff grass and soil stuck to her back. And the air,
swelling with pollen, blurs at the edges as more men
move their arms in what's become a ritual gesture
in this field where even grass has become a conspiracy
you want to believe isn't a murmur of green, but more
a moan, like the man's tongue finds in the woman's body.

Or the almost white shriek this field becomes dusted with snow.
The way it was the day in February a boy found the body
of a woman with a crevice where her face should have been.
There was snow on what was left of her clothes, but her skin
was still warm enough to turn the crystal lyric of water

back into its more mundane nature. The boy knelt down to
brush the snow from the cloth that wound over the woman
like a shroud and, though he didn't think to do it,
and for twenty years he wouldn't remember, he touched
the cold-raised nipples of the corpse with his tongue.

It's while the almost white curves of the baseballs make lines
through the pollen of this field in summer that you remember
the bland taste of that quiet flesh. How the cold ridges of
skin seemed the map of a country you couldn't yet name,
but knew you'd fall into someday. The glove on your hand
is wet and beginning to itch. You want to pull it off,
but the sweltering air is as full of baseballs as pollen,
and they're moving so fast the stitches are blurred scars.
You're afraid if one struck your ungloved hand it would break skin
and leave a ragged scar like a letter naming the past.
You're afraid of even the stray thought of one being hit
with a bat. It could open down herringbone seams and release
other bodies lost in the uncut fields of grass gone to seed,
in memory. You see, through a haze of hurled baseballs,
the torso and unmarred head of the woman risen above
the seed-burdened stems of dry grass. The man is buried in
a memory of his own, the woman straddling his prone body
almost replaced by another woman. There are so many
baseballs in the air no one could count them, and you want to
walk over to the seed-covered woman saying the name
of a man and lick the pollen and sweat from her back.

But the air is off-white and dangerous, and distance is a voice
you imagine is the echo of the last breath of the woman
whose breasts invited you into this dream where you are
paralyzed by the memory and loss thrown by the sore arms
of figures who have donned old gloves in the sunlight
visible in the raw drift of pollen. So much grief,
and so much pleasure, has been played out in the subtle
impressions of bodies still barely articulate in this grass
you believe is as innocent as a reservoir, the body
of a woman wavering in its water, luminous
pollen settling on algae the texture of a woman's hair
tangled from turning in her sleep or the crosshatching of grass
matted down by bodies. Of water, you'd like to say
it's a comfort. That if you could reach the public fountain
the water you'd swallow would be cold and uncontaminated
by even the memory of flesh. It would come from

a reservoir surrounded by reedy grass, the kind that hides
most anything. Of innocence, you'd like to say nothing
comes of it. That no matter where anything begins,
it always comes back to blurs in the air that could be baseballs,
or pollen, or something as unreliable as memory.
You can hear Claire Lejeune, in a room where smoke curls
in the rhythm of her voice as though it were a lover
or the calm surface of a body of cold water, saying
The ultimate object of human fear is Beauty. The only way
out of this field of grass that goes on dying, being crushed
into impressions of the bodies of lovers and children playing,
is to accept the fact the past is a gauze that is stitched
to our flesh. And every gesture of longing that does no damage,
even the drift of a boy's tongue on the cool skin
of a reservoir or the body of a woman raped and murdered
and dumped in a field of dead grass whitening
in a late February snow, every gentle touch,
is an act of contrition in the pollen, and a prayer
your body writes to praise what you still call beauty.

The brilliant bodies, scarred and sweaty, of the baseballs
curve past you into other gloves covered with cursive letters
you imagine are drafts of a story someone's still revising,
or perhaps the frantic prayer written after the first death.
The woman and the man have dressed and stand on mowed grass
in the haze of pollen past where baseballs fill the air.
This close, you recognize them and know what's beginning
in her body, the embrace of solid and fluid. You are
beginning. And the woman whose body had floated face down
in the cold water of the reservoir has turned over
and is laughing. Fooled you, she says, her almost naked form
convincing you it's time to wake up. To embrace the woman
sleeping beside you, her body a whispered matin for beauty
that can let you ignore the baseballs and forget the pollen
and all its echoes, except the goosepimpled flesh
of the woman who's played a prank and leads you back
to the field of uncut grass where the vague impression
of both your bodies hums with the mating call
of some insect. You remember being afraid of
something, but her body, covered in pollen, is real
enough to confess everything to. And you do.

ANIMALS HOUSED IN THE PLEASURE OF FLESH

Forgetfulness is useful to the preservation of the individual.
—Paul Éluard

1.
Our breath rose becoming,
with distance, only air,
an elegy written by bodies
which long for touch
the way some insects crave
our thick blood. Memory
is air too thin to live on.
Canaries would die breathing it,
their vibrant yellow bodies
giving up on song. Memory
would have music coming from
a car radio clear of static.
She had caught a sleeve of
her linen blouse on a low branch,
the snag a white scar
I smoothed out, an excuse
for touch, her pale flesh
a body of faith that required
more prayer than the breath
my lungs could hold. Memory
would burn that sleeve
into my flesh like a wing,
the snag becoming the white breath
of her naked body, the music
I can't remember. Now,
a woman often sings me
to sleep with Welsh songs,
a foreign music to placate
my heart after sex, to end it
imagining blood getting thinner.
The heart, despite its bravado,
is thick with guilt. After all,
there is blood on its breath.

2.
Grass was a pale gray stain
rooted in a loam the barest of layers
for our bodies. Rock took over
at a shallow depth we thought

41

we could dig to with our hands.
Below the last million years
of stone, men labored.
Our breath rose toward
a scattered light as much the past
as the dust men breathed in
under the earth. When we were
finished, birds crossed through
what was left of our breath.
They were only grackles,
but their flared boat-tails left
a wake in the dark we were
sure we could follow home.

3.
Hard-shelled black beetles woke
under our wet bodies,
our lungs longing for ellipses
of air. What remains
is the sad taste of blood
where she bit my lip,
her body becoming a light
that made visible the simple,
elegant figures of animals
housed in the pleasure of flesh.
When my tongue touches the scar,
I wonder where she is.

4.
In Wales, men know the ritual
of looking in rock for what is
needed. They know what breaks
between one word and the next,
having kissed the bodies of men
whose swollen lungs had burst
under the earth. They know memory
needs solid beams of oak
to shore it up. They know the hearts
of birds, held loose, hum in black
fingers. They could break
with the loss of sky. Birds don't
sing the same after the mines.
Even the barest breath of gas
changes them. An old miner
once told me, *The gas reminds them
what they're singing about.*

Maybe air just plays their bodies
like flutes through scarred lungs.
Or maybe the hearing changes,
not the song. Maybe something
rises in the blood of men
coming back to the country of air,
the way nitrogen bubbles form
in the blood of divers who rise
too fast from places where water
won't allow light. Places
where fish burn their own flesh
to find food so they can go on
burning to find food. Maybe
the black dust that burns
men's lungs until breath is a pain
they long to endure
isn't an illness, but a ballad,
their ruined bodies the notes
that score it. Maybe
the black bile they'll cough up
is like the burning part
of a fish that never sees
any light but what it makes.

5.
Flesh, a sign, burns and is not
consumed, pain a flowering
from a layer of ash and soil
that goes deeper than we could
dig to. The past
rises from damp ground. It was
rising the night her pale skin became
real. People speak of burning
moments into memory, as if
a lithograph could be burned
into the landscape, into soil
and down to the rock men carve
tunnels in, burned into the rock
and the air trapped in it
so the last thing a scared man sees
before his lungs expand past
the point of flesh is the form
of two bodies entangled.
Seeing this, he might think
of his wife. How two nights before
the collapse, he was in her

and she chanted his name. But
this isn't what he thinks of. There
isn't enough oxygen to think
of anything as real as this. Memory,
no matter what we say it is,
or should be, remains personal.
She said all around us the elms
were dying, the hard-edged cells
burning. Even the dead
limbs could hold us, though,
she said. She wanted to
climb into the dying wound
of wood and sleep, held
from the predictable damp grass
in the morning. She said
it would wake the dead memories
in our cells. Why was I afraid
of lying with her among the dead
branches? What would
the morning have been if I had?
Not even the dead can answer,
no matter how precise the words
meant to summon them back
from their own concerns.
The old sacrifices don't work,
and the dead can't tell us
what we'd have to do
to reach them now.

6.
Even air has limits. It can be forced
miles below rock to form
caverns of oxygen, dust flowering
in the currents, lungs dark petals
curved round the one true stamen
of blood which blooms red
only in the country of air.
And air longs to love the body,
to know flesh as more
than a translation from a language
it can't speak. We are proof
air loves, the flowering of blood
around a wound only the body
offering the air a gift. But
air doesn't know the loss
that lies under flesh, a taproot

twisting deep in the body.
And no air can know the lines
drawn in the body's dark
that form memory, which is
more than images of animals
locked in gray and dying
cells, more than any air
could stand. Brought back up
to the light it shines dark
enough to make any soul
collapse, and swear
nothing could be more pure.

7.
We can't go down into the body.
Whatever may be etched,
or burned like soot, on the pale
walls of bone that keep
this illusion of flesh
from caving in, we have to
live in fields our bodies
lie down in. Fields where
the dark forms of grackles
move sharp like sickles over
acres of rape, the yellow
an unreal setting for birds
so black. No, we can't go down
into the body. Not even
to bring back to the surface
bodies we've touched and whispered
the names of in rooms
where flesh was a kind of light.
These bodies rise, and we can
pretend we've called them, a lie
to comfort us. The canaries
we dream fling fragile bones
against our warm bodies,
yellow feathers drifting in currents
of sour sleep-breath,
and grackles click bitter histories
in our limbs. When we wake
to find our bodies sore,
our skin almost a pain,
we shouldn't blame blood denied
but the frantic aviary
of our night flesh, the hungry

throats that fly sooty air
over fields we can't lie down in.

8.
Begin with breath rising
into a memory of breath.
A rosary of two wet bodies
moving together in a field,
color drained from flesh and grass.
Imagine birds nearby
small as wrens, the nuances
of grays. Imagine the two
lie still, finally, in the vague
form of love beaten down
in grass. Imagine a car
passes by, the driver unaware
how close he is to a place
where flesh is recovering
from what passion requires,
the rush of blood away
from the brain. Imagine
the windows are down,
on the radio an old Welsh song
about a grove of ash
where the dead return
with music and kind faces. Imagine
how that music sounds
to the man and the woman coming back
to their bodies in the grass.
Imagine there's no such thing
as memory, that even the past
moves off from us at speeds
we can't calculate. The song
on the radio is one a woman
sings to me in bed. Imagine
breath is a rosary,
each inhalation a bead
to finger as prayer leaves
the flesh. Imagine memory
is an issue of faith.

9.
To believe what happened
happened is to live
in the places flesh forms
and to believe in singing,

whether of birds or the woman
lying next to me in bed.
To believe her breath blesses
my hand inches from her mouth.
I don't mean to wake her.
I mean to go on feeling
her breath on my palm,
to not confuse this woman
with any other woman,
this breath with any other breath.
To keep from using the actual
suffering of any man
or woman for anything less
than what they've become.
I mean to deny nothing.
To let all the dark birds
we ignore punctuate memory,
as if what's remembered
needs a grammar of its own.
I mean to let these awkward
black birds congregate
in yellow fields of rape,
and believe they forgive me
any sin words might make of them.
To believe the music
their hearts would hum
if I held them in this hand
warmed by the breath
of a sleeping woman
would be a Welsh tune
sung by the last miner
left in a collapsed shaft,
the air thinning around him
and in his lungs,
his own heart a bird
on an ashen branch
beginning to sing,
or a hesitant angel bursting,
finally, into psalm,
or just an old wound
that reminds him how the breath
of a woman filled
his body with blood.

10.

My wife murmurs in her sleep.
The words could be another language,
or it could be the distance
they've had to travel
to reach someone still awake
has made them dark birds
with calls that sound like punctuation.
There is no telling the sentences
they end, no way to know
if there's enough air left in my lungs
to call her back from the country
she has gone to. A place
where birds return each year
to elaborate festivals
and papier-mâché replicas
that are exact in every detail.
People dance around the dark figures
of what could be taken for gods.
Everyone's at the parade,
even the men cradling in
their laps the bags which fill
their collapsed lungs with air.
Women wheel them to the front
of the crowds lining the streets,
and the small yellow birds
their faces have become
open their beaks as if the air
were thick enough to peck
whole chunks off to swallow.
After the parade is over
and the men have been lifted
out of wheelchairs into beds,
after their wives have stripped
them of everything but
their bags of air and straddled
their boney bodies and moved
over them, their open palms
warm on the loose skin
of concave chests, stopping now
and then to listen
to the breathing of the men
they love, after the women
have cleaned themselves
and their husbands with the warmth
of damp washcloths, after

the woman have fallen asleep
carefully beside the damaged bodies
of these men who have spent
much of their lives under
the earth, the men lie awake in
that country and listen to the reason
the birds have returned.
All night the men sip
from their clear bags of air
while the bitter sound
of feathered bodies
entering one another goes on
until the air they breathe
seems thinner than ever
and they fall asleep clutching
the bags to their chests.
When they dream, these men
living in the country
whose native tongue is the murmuring
of my sleeping wife,
they dream of a place where the air
never runs out, where
there's so much sky
even the papier-mâché birds
could begin to sing.
To believe in what happened
is to stroke the stiff,
wrinkled chest of a bird-idol
and imagine the song
that comes out of that chest
formed of ripped paper and glue
is the breath of a woman
warm on the open palm I hold
inches from her mouth.
To imagine memory
is such breath, and that
I could place my open mouth
over hers and breathe
a whole country of air
and remembered air where grackles
and wrens and canaries
fly over two bodies held together
by sweat and the faith
they will remember any of this.

A faith that scorches stone
near the delicate lines of animals,
and says the place
their flesh has formed in
the grass will remain.

Dark birds I didn't know the name of danced
in tepid water. I asked a local woman
with dark skin what the birds were. She told me
the Spanish name, a word like locusts,
like a curse, like nothing I'd use for those birds
that were everywhere, like grackles in Ohio,
the inhuman crack of their voices
almost a blessing from throats that swallow dust
that could be history or an old sorrow
laid out like ash. Their voices might have been
curses, or prayers. Or the voice of a woman
whose throat was a wound of sand. Her hands
caressed distance out of my back and legs
when she could touch me without the brown body
of anyone's despair or rage taking flight.
She often spoke of the house her father filled
with tribal masks whose sour breath clouded
the rooms. At night, their lips spoke demons
she didn't want to find a way into her.

In Austin, where the landscape is spoken
by old voices, I remembered dreaming
a voice for the masks that spoke of her
body. Their breath in those dreams was mine,
moving over her flesh like dust, or sorrow.
But this woman didn't belong any place
in the Southwest. She's a memory. Not even
her voice is real, unless what's uttered
by the carved lips of sleep can be said
to be real. Memory clings to places
like a time-scarred insect. Think of locusts.
Imagine the sporadic leaping of bodies
in dark clouds. The voracious hunger. The curse
of the insect body, the bones a private hell
to burn in. The past is not a place,
or it's a field consumed by insects. The masks,
whose breath stained the plaster of a house
in Ohio, could have been carved by tribes
whose flesh was darkened by living
in Austin before it had that name. Perhaps
the woman who only knew the Spanish name
for the brown jays held in her DNA
the elegant gestures of hands over wood

to form images for the voices of gods. Perhaps
she could've led me to some dark adobe room
and undressed while tepid water moved
through pipes. Perhaps her hands would have
carved my face into a faint semblance of some god
she might have whispered the name of.
And it might have been the Spanish word
she had used to name the birds. The past
is not a place, unless it's where words
like *perhaps* remember flesh. In the language
of tribes who burned the carved faces
of gods, *perhaps* could be a curse
or a prayer, depending on a gesture of hands.

The only fragments of their language are inked
on clay vessels kept dry in glass cases
in the Southwest, or carved on masks
in rooms in Ohio. No one living has heard
the language, but one morning in Austin
a woman in a dream held a tribal mask in front of
her face and breathed a word I couldn't
make out. Awake, I'd have risen naked
to form an echo of the carved sign in
that forgotten language for *memory*. Instead,
still half-dreaming in a damp shroud,
I listened to local insects chirr themselves
mad at the return of light and thought it
a lamentation for the wounded, dying
body of history, which is not the past,
but the pale flesh of sorrow that won't stay
in the past. No matter what inked symbol
my body echoed in some awkward position
it took in sleep, any voice whispered in
memory is false, a vague water stain on sheets
that echoes the intricate, carved shape of desire,
which the body only forms part of. Perhaps
the matins of the birds whose Spanish name
is more a curse than a prayer could bless
the barren and faceless walls in any house.

Perhaps memory is the body's matins and vespers,
and the faith such prayers require has been carved
in the forms of faces and birds. I want to know
the name of the brown jays in a language
no one living can read or speak that was chanted
through the carved lips of masks painted

the colors of dust. A complex hand gesture
made it the name of a bird and not
the word said to a lover when the body is sore
with distance and needs the slow motion of hands
carving small circles over knotted muscles. Said
with a different gesture, the word which named
the brown jays could mean the moon's a memory,
a stain in the sky where it's been swallowed
by a creature no one's ever seen more of
than its head. Which was worn certain nights
by a woman who'd dance barefoot in warm ashes,
chanting through the mask, and choose
a man she'd lead into the desert to a cave
where she'd carve his body in passion and leave
scripture in the scars to serve as memory
for everyone who read his flesh. Neither
would remember what had happened in the cave,
which had a name. *Dark where the body
wakens*, or, closer, *Womb of forgetting.*
Any translation is a voice in memory,
or a stain on sheets, the faint aura
left behind by the pleasures of bodies.

A forgotten language still clings, like a shell
of some short-lived insect, to the walls of caves
in the desert outside Austin, where lovers
have touched words they didn't recognize
with their naked flesh, and the fading memories
of hands pressed to bodies have responded
in kind to the chants left in the amnesia
of passion. Old folks have come with lanterns
to copy the words. Huddled in their worn bodies,
they've known, in some way the body has of knowing,
what's been done in those scorched and sacred places,
and in whose names. Perhaps the woman
who named the birds with what could have been
a curse or a god might have led me
to one of those caves in the desert and touched
my body in the old ways. Perhaps it wouldn't have
taken scars but just a willingness to remember,
and a faith in the prayer the body knows
as sorrow to name what needs to be
named in a language we speak, not knowing
the words. Back in Ohio, I think of
the brown jays. How one morning I fed one
missing a leg, amazed at how it clung

fierce along an iron fence and hopped
the red, baked tiles after torn bread. How
it could beat the others to the ragged bits.
And the memory of that bird comes to me
like a blessing, like the touch of a pale hand
on a body older than it is, speaking
a language older than the forgotten tongue
in caves outside Austin. The language the body,
always memory, is carved of, and carves.

In homes near the center of town,
men have faith in the scarred promises
of religion, and every night
suffer their wives' sleep. Water surges
in the calm air above the fountain
of a goddess sculpted in the pale arms
of her husband, Death. The rumor of
the spray drifts over them and cools
their dream flesh. Wolves roam the edge of
town, starved and sounding like jealousy.
All day, Lakota sit on rusted chains
and smoke in front of the used car lot,
whispering to the gray and black wolves.

The gray stone cut out of local mountains
to build the courthouse is being cleaned,
sandblasted by men with masks
who curse the pain in their lungs despite
the cloth. Lakota avoid the viscous dust.
The wolves are hungrier, and come
further in to town. Men who work late shifts
breathe the dust in their sleep. In Waking,
no one believes the wolves are any more
dangerous than the dark tinge on the stone.

The stain is as clear a sign as they are
likely to get that ruin has a name,
and a husband, but not her husband's name.
And if the wolves are a reminder
of what they've lost, the dust that flies off
the stone is evidence that even in Waking
faith is all in the pitch. The goddess
comes to everyone except the Lakota
in dreams. They watch her sell used cars
at noon, promises made over relics
drifting along the form of her body
like a rumor of dust dreaming it's water.

Or water dreaming it's dust. Waking,
the Lakota might say, is built over
sacred ground, the used car lot at night
covered by the souls of ancestors
in the jealous guise of wolves. Slashed tires

found mornings are pictographs,
voices of the dead that speak of the curse
that follows living. In town, children
draw stick figures over the tracks of wolves
who seem to dance some aberrant waltz.

And scars heal exactly how scars heal
in any town. The carved fountain attracts
nondescript birds people feed without
thinking, the water permission to care
for everything. When a car passes,
the birds rise from the pavement, a sleep
disturbed by the hunger of motion,
jealousy dusting the air with what could be
echoes of a waltz played too much
in the fashion of a dirge. The Lakota
recognize the tune as an old one,
and hum it to soothe the wolves' despair.

With such music suffering the air
it's easy to feel abandoned, to imagine
the goddess is a real woman
who used to live in Waking but left
years ago to visit a darkened country
where the mountains aren't gray and speak
a different tongue. When she didn't
return, the town council commissioned
a local Lakota artist to carve her
out of native stone. It was his
idea to make her Persephone,
Hades the scarred body of a man
whose chest was once opened by wolves.

The dust, jealous of the stone, leaves
a veil the goddess wears everywhere
water's too cursed to reach. The story of
the statue's a lie. Everyone knows it.
The woman whose form it remembers
is the sculptor's wife. Rumor is
he caught her one afternoon with
the man whose arms now confine her
in stone, a man whose name was
a mournful howl out of the mountains
no one could imitate. Every scar
that marks any body adds to the dust

the goddess hums under, to the sore
music scored by children in dirt.

Or to the lies the Lakota know
are lies that everyone believes.
Like the wolves. To begin with,
there've been no wolves in Waking
for almost sixty years. And yet
there are the tracks, and the music
men make out of the breath of women
asleep. A music something moves to,
furtively, among the pine trees
that shade all the roads out of town.
And everyone believes it's wolves
the Lakota whisper to, not something
as mundane as memory. The stain
is a sign, they say. They don't know
what's coming, but they believe it
isn't just the dust carved off stone.

No one knows what the Lakota believe.
Some mornings, one of the old ones
washes the windows of the showroom
on the used car lot. If you stand
at just the right distance, you'll see in
the dark glass a reflection, not his
but a cross between a man and a wolf.
It will be an illusion, a trick
of light, but for that moment
you'll believe even the goddess is
possible. You will believe even a man
covered in dust and carved out of stone
can hold a woman in Waking
with enough passion to heal them both,
and long enough to become a god.

from Attendant Ghosts

A monk moved in over me and the room stayed bare.
Light, he said with rum and good jazz, needs space.
It's hard to listen to a monk talk about need.
For confession, he said, to be more than a drunk,
stumbling through fog-ridden fields of corn
or sleeping it off in barns where lame cows low
a mournful music, the rum can't be watered down
and Thelonious has to be loud enough for the woman
down the hall who cooks sausage and peppers Sundays
to hum in perfect pitch with the piano.
                                        The last time
I held a Bible, I swore to tell the whole truth.
With no confession, they'd said, my testimony
was all they had. I lied and she walked. And danced
with me that night in a bar where guilt was a song
someone kept picking on the jukebox, her body
a prayer the monk, mute from drink and the grace
of flesh, chanted later in the devotional glow
of candles. Every witness recanted, claimed whiskey
as excuse, and started gossiping about how lame
cows were wandering, hobbled, blocking the traffic
this town had yet to lose. The monk prayed for
the bones, arthritic, to heal, the milk to be coveted
and hoarded against the fear of drought, knowing
there's a long history of neglect and violence in town,
that jazz plays in refurbished bars where drunks swear
they smell sausage and peppers and remember
touching girls in the dark behind organs playing hymns
the congregation choked on.
                             Some evenings the monk
played a piano, the music collapsing under
his hands, and I'd think of a girl my friends called
a cow. I touched her once, huge in a pew
at morning mass. My hand went to sleep under her
thigh, and was still tingling when the priest slipped
the flesh of Christ into my palm, my own brand
of stigmata. I touched her on a dare, never confessed.
She's become a grotesque in the itinerate circus
of the past. A clown shouts her name out of his
comic flesh no colors disguise the sorrow of. Acrobats
convince me that touch is true faith, the way
they hover in air, absolution. The freaks,
who feed animals with threadbare skins, believe

their hands can stroke that flesh into a music
that could cure a crippled form. Accompanied by
scratched records of Monk turning simple scales
into manna, they pray.
      Maybe the girl I touched
in that pew is thin now, and her lover's an acrobat,
his shoulder blades pale scars. When they make love,
he thinks of flying over fields of cows who low a music
of loss and sway their massive heads as if in prayer.
Her delicate hands drift over his back like wings,
the way Thelonious touched a piano. The way he was
said to be touched by desperate angels. The jukebox
in the bar where I danced with an angel has one
Monk song. When it plays I feel the need to touch
a woman who could make my hands a prayer
in some room with a scratched piano and a Bible
left open to Revelations, the monk gone, the rum
tasting of dust and the lassitude of cows. Even jazz
can't make violence or the memory of neglect an excuse
for any of this.
      Some nights, I imagined the thirsty
creak of a trapeze in the attic room, believing the cross
an acrobat's body formed meant forgiveness was possible
even in this world. I wanted to touch again the body
of the woman who laid herself down in dust to watch
a human cross hover. Some mornings there's an outline
in the dust on my bed, but no matter what I confess
lying in that vague recollection of a body, no music
forgives me, or the woman who left the acrobat
for a man who made her believe she was a prayer
he needed to chant to live. Say it was the monk,
that he believed her body was a circus where light
performed acrobatics no one in the crowd would
forget, that truth limped outside the tent, a lame cow,
its low lifting the dust lit by a klieg light towards
an acrobat swaying in a drunk haze just before
he confesses his love for gravity and begins to fall.

You could die in this bar, or be born again, maybe
the preacher on the corner who clutches his chest
and collapses into chant. A woman could forgive
drink and the bitter rasp of your breath asleep,
if you could hang a solid beam level. Or confess
every hurt on knees that creak like the rafters
in the cathedral where a boy sang whose voice
was as brittle as the martyred saint made of glass,
a body blooming arrows the way he imagined
his would, touched by a woman. Even Christ
knew drink was the way in, every saint a drunk,
cathedrals nothing without wine, just stained light
and the trick with mirrors they call forgiveness.
Like Joseph, you build things out of wood,
and sawdust drifts inside you and settles on
a town where every building remembers
your hands and won't collapse. You pray to
the blurred mirrors in this bar, and forgive
every woman who took back touch.
                                    You could love
in this bar, enough to go back to that graying,
weathered church and sing a hymn with the boy
who aches and believes a woman could slur
his name with cheap wine and erase everything.
To sin, the preacher on the corner shouts,
leaves sawdust in the heart. To forgive yourself,
give the boy a tour of the town you've built.
Let him kick up the sawdust like leaves,
or pack it in his small, unscarred hands like snow
and build a man who could love a woman
without anything piercing his skin.
                                    This bar
needs a statue of Saint Sebastian bristling
in a corner, lit so the arrows seem to quiver
with songs about heartache and whiskey
someone keeps paying for. A woman
could pull the arrows out, breathe over the holes
in the plaster saint and play a tune you would
remember from church. A drunk collapsed
at the bar would sing with the angelic voice
of a choir boy who believed that to love
a woman, even one who could breathe a hymn
out of the suffering body of a saint in a bar,

63

you have to listen, sober, to the psalms
of her breath, each saint a different hymn.
With them all, you could build a cathedral
nothing could be doubted in, where the light
would be the body's breath blooming in a rage
of wine and mirrors.
      To die in this bar, love
a woman, and let the arrows in with the music
her body makes or pays for, the corner jukebox
an open wound. No psalm can praise touch
enough to carve a heart in the wall. No song can
make you a saint or a drunk, or carve your face
in wood over a tormented body, a confession
of arrows and love. And if you pray
in this bar, no one will hear you who could
answer. Not a lost choirboy. Not even
a woman whose touch could sober a saint.

It's how birds mimic the horse's mane, strung in the dead elm
in the background, how their songs dismiss questions the sky
might ask if it were pretending it cares how any of this turns
out. It's only that there are some common birds lifting,
an afterthought, into the nonchalant sky. Maybe it is
none of this. Maybe someone thought no one would notice
the birds, or the woman's fingers merging with the horse's mane.
Maybe the grackles, caught in an instant defining abandon
as a verb, are an accident, and the figures foregrounded
by what's possible through the careful use of focus are enough

to create the illusion of history and give license to ignore
the startling line of what are only common birds. Maybe
this is a statement about our being condemned, our sentence
that not one of us can name the beautiful woman who longs
to confess everything to the horse and climb on and ride
out of the subdued grays of this photograph. The lifting
grackles turn to follow her, and the jagged line of their flight
records the vague rhythm of a sore and bitter heart. Irregular,
it points to the frayed ends of this sky that can't keep up
its pretense through all the chemicals. Everything that was

supposed to be in focus is blurred and leans out of the photo.
There's a name for how the tasseled corn in the background drifts
through the almost solid bodies that would be the point of this.
So often, what passes through us is someone on a horse, bareback
and blurred. The figures with names want to become more and more
anonymous, while the woman and the line of dark birds refuse
to forget the heart's been drawn on sheer cliffs as a horse half
human, its torso tattooed with a naked woman whose name
was written in letters so small the painted rock has absorbed
every trace over the years. The heart ignores any sign

of mimicry in the ragged line of grackles lifting from a tree
no one's carved a woman's name in. The nondescript bark
is a record of storms and the history of indifference.
If it wasn't blurred, the scars of weather would tell of the day
one April a woman pressed her back against it and made the sky
jealous. A man tore off her clothes and burned her blank skin
with a branding iron until her throat was a confession
that flicked the scabbed and fly-burdened ears of horses
in the stable the woman could almost see through the smoke
that had been her flesh. Focus doesn't let such history in,

and nothing disturbs the illusion everything's composed.
The woman with the horse never knew how the scars, letters
on her mother's sad breasts, got there, but her first words
were her attempts to pronounce that red braille of raised flesh.
Her mother cried when she spoke, language a mime of grief
until it's spoken. Then, it gallops through our bodies and blurs
the signs we make to name what we love. Maybe the grackles
aren't lifting from the elm, but settling in its branches,
tired of an indifferent sky. Maybe verbs are never sure.
Maybe the horse is the point of this, the only thing not left.

A blind man, hands gnarled and numb from years
of smoking, walks by. Amnesic clouds stumble
in a sky that could stack the deck without us

catching on. The evening has that edge
of despair that croaks the blues. Across
this lot, the weathered blinds left open

let anyone see a ripped and faded print
of Edward Hopper's *Office at Night*.
Longing keeps the man's hands fanatic

with reports long since lost, instead of
praying over the stark flesh of this woman
he can't bear to see without the intimacy

of touch. Maybe desire and ash both drift
in the air of the office. Any minute,
Josephine could kiss his hand from the canvas.

It's her body that translates this dress
into an argument against forgetting. Her flesh
whispers, *Leave the world to burn itself*

down. Any minute, the young couple
arguing in the parking lot could
forget where they are and touch without

the blues turning anything in the world
to ash. The sky could make silos in
the distance disappear into the threat

of some nameless storm. Where land is
worn down and ignored, no wind stays
long enough to be personal. But in this

frozen office, the woman's ankles are pure
and poised, and no one could ever fall
down but to kiss them. Josephine

poses in painting after painting, nude
or dressed in clothes functional at best.
In fluorescent light, every tone of flesh

67

emerges, innocent, like hymns blind men
sing alone in their beds with every kind
of dark drifting inside and around them.

Hopper said it was light, not
the bodies or barren walls, he loved.
The light, he said, was what he was

painting. And every story he made color
and form and composition whisper
had to do with distance. Light goes

a long way just to become something else.
Where does this couple think they are
headed? Maybe they want to believe

weather can't blind them. Maybe they want
to make love in an office at night
and not care about the reports that drift

out the open window into the dark
air ten stories up, how they'd seem
almost to be ashes if anyone

passing by looked up. Josephine,
not even light is innocent now.
And the couple is gone, driving

down a darkening road in a car
dented and scratched and missing
a headlight. They are forgetting

the argument and how it seemed ash
filled their mouths. They are forgetting
the sky and how the absence of light

suggests rain longs to lose itself in
the legacy of their sore bodies,
in any landscape so open it could

sing the blues to a wind desperate enough
to caress something so worn down
and bitter. They are forgetting how

history is blind enough to need
to touch stone or bodies to remember
what happened, enough to imagine ash

is something to write in without loss.
Josephine, forget everything
but the way this blue dress argues for

your body. Step out of it and sing
Edward from the canvas. Sing his hands
onto your flesh, with the blind touch

of a lover who denies the easy mistake
of despair. Sing the couple into
whatever office they can touch in

without losing anything, not even
themselves. Josephine, believe your voice
can turn even ash into desire.

MADDENED BY INSECTS AND STRANGE HYMNS

Wind this wild has always brought them freaks.
—Richard Hugo

Freaks have raised tents at the edge of town
where I once kissed a woman. Men pay
sad coins to stare at them and ignore how
they'll kiss demented tonight and dance
on fire in klieg lights across the field

I confessed love in. The woman said
she wanted to crawl inside me. No field
is more blessed. No matter it's freaks dancing.
Grass doesn't know the difference, and wind
will touch them like the music I waste quarters

to hear in this bar where old men talk of women
they loved, their hearts so heavy no light
can escape. Inside tents staked in damp soil,
stages have been hammered together by pale men
with gills that open and close as if singing

a sad tune in praise of kisses that burn long
enough to make the moon blush. Garish posters
make the faint of heart blush all over town.
Believe, they say, your eyes. Nothing but the truth
can make me feel that sad coin in my chest

I keep paying out for the music a woman sang
beside me after we made love in a field
where, tonight, people won't believe their eyes.
They'll hold familiar bodies and try not to cringe
when the woman with the open chest drops her robe

and her heart beats in front of them, a rosetta stone
no one will decipher. Though she'll talk to everyone
who stops to look, the only one she'll invite back
after things close down is the blind boy
who reaches out to touch what he can't believe. Braille

is another language of doubt and pleasure. She wants
his fingers to close up the wound and let her love

70

being a woman no one would look twice at.
Days after the freaks have left, the blind boy will
put up posters with awkward letters that offer

a large reward for any reliable information
about love. Without knowing it, he'll put his
scrawled pleas over the carnival's tawdry posters.
Tonight, a woman will wander drunk into a tent
marked Closed and find a man crying. When

she touches his shoulder, his body will ripple
like the surface of the local, stagnant lake
couples park beside to hold someone and breathe
something they can't name. He'll look up at her,
his face a hundred mouths swirling in

such frenzy he can't make one articulate sound.
The ripple from her touch will cross over his face
and his mouths will settle long enough for him to say
Thank you before he's water again. She'll bend down
and kiss as many mouths as she can. Later

she'll swear it was like drowning without fear.
She'll think no one believes her, but I will.
Others will say the freaks don't stay put but wander
outside the tents, humming a sad song that drives
insects into a frenzy. One man will swear

he knows the song but can't place it. I'll buy him
another beer and he'll try to hum what drifted in
the air maddened by insects and a strange hymn.
No one expects to hear something they'd have said
belonged to them coming from throats so wrong,

like the man whose hands are starlings. Story is
he loved a woman so much he wanted his touch
to be a song, to make her fly away from her life,
and when she said she'd never love him his hands
started to sing from dark throats and his fingers

were wings. Women go home after seeing him
and dream his hands flying over their backs,
their legs, and cling to the men who don't know
what's gotten into them and turn their backs
to these women imagining the flight of

71

touch. The blind boy will whisper to the birds
he feeds in the park. *Her heart*, he'll say, *was
no freak.* He'll say how, when he least expects it,
it's there in his hand. The birds will sing her heart
under the dark skies old men will say have come

to stay after the carnival leaves. I'll hear the song
and want to head out after the freaks, to catch up
at the next town and pay sad coins to believe.
Or dream of a woman whose eyes are maddening
swirls of color the sign outside her tent says

can tell the future. In the dream, she'll see me
and cover her eyes with hands that could be screams
and I'll wake to birds outside, their wings
now and then grazing the window. The sound will
almost make me believe any touch can heal

the most crippled flesh. Tonight, in the bar,
the couples who come back from seeing the freaks
will sit close in the dark booths and touch the flesh
they love because it's what they expect. To find
what love can do to the body, all I'd need

to do is stop putting coins in the jukebox
and head out to where the woman I kissed
bit my lip and left a scar in the shape of
some drifting bird of prey. Over the tents
flapping in wind coming in hard from the north,

I'd see the dark edge of a storm and believe
wherever you go you can't trust weather. I would
step sober into a sad tent with no sign. A woman
would gesture me closer. Somewhere, gills
in men's necks would play the blues. She would

wrap around me and kiss me. I'd realize
she has no bones, and feel something like despair
just under her skin, but nothing more solid.
*The phosphorus in bones could be where love forms
first*, she'd whisper as her soft flesh cried around

my body. Tonight, the bar will seem broken
somehow, the beer watered-down and bitter.
Couples will do shots over memories of freaks

72

dancing in a light that could have come from
the bones of the dead bickering under the grass

insects rise from, mating in clouds of their own
burning. Fireflies are freaks. They stagger
in the dark as if they're drunk and the moon is
a conspiracy of light that wants
to confuse them. The woman I kissed

where freaks dance in the madness of light
left years ago. Any mark she made in my flesh isn't
something I could show freaks for pity. Unless
I could invite them in to the bitter cloister
of the abandoned monastery in my chest. Maybe

they would have names for the misshapen
animals that limp strange dances and whimper
through the dust that won't settle in the halls.
Maybe the woman without a mouth could sign names
for the birds that flap obscenely from room

to room, not able to quite get off the ground.
Her hands would be a lesson of grace the birds
would mimic if they could and to fly. Maybe
I'd kiss her fingers and something that could be
a deer would panic and bump over and over

a stained-glass window, trying to get out through
Christ healing a leper. I'd let her hands go
and they'd calm the frantic animal and write words
on its coat, whole sentences I'd swear were mine.
Maybe I'd try to kiss her a mouth and not tell

later what moved under the skin where it wasn't.
I'd just drink whiskey and listen to the blind boy
rant until a woman put his hand under her blouse
and he sobbed for what he'd never feel again.
Tonight, he'll go back to the carnival after it's closed

and not heal anything. Tonight, I'll try to
comfort a woman whose mouth is sore from kissing
so many mouths. She'll barely be able to swallow
the pale wine paid for with the last of the coins
I'd meant to slip into the jukebox. The last

sad song I picked will be playing. When she touches
my neck to be sure I'm not water, I'll be
humming the pain out of the song. I'll believe
nothing will ever lock back up the freaks
the carnival let out. The couples will slow dance

to the music. Their uncorrupted bodies will
translate pain into love, or someone will
stumble through me and leave the bar penniless
for the edge of town, where tents shudder in
rain, and a woman mourns the moon and a kiss.

The minaret's been missing for months. Cows
devout and solemn in the sparse corn fields
have their brand of prayer, and chew their cud slow
out of respect. Loss takes on many forms.
No one's left out. I imagine wind is
responsible. In town, people know wind
by its family name. No one bothers to
get more familiar. Wind's not invited
anywhere. It just shows up, loud and drunk
and feeling us up until we shudder.

No one knows who gives the wind alcohol.
All the owners of taverns in town say
nothing's missing when they inventory
after storms. Still, I picture a drunk wind
staggering through corn with the lonely roof
of a minaret. I want it to mean
something, this awkward dance. Religion is
what broke the bitter man who drinks whiskey
every night and ends up cursing the bar
before dancing through abandoned streets home.

I've heard he was once a priest. *Love isn't
all it's cracked up to be*, he likes to say,
sometimes shouting it from the street, waking
me to stand at the window and watch him
stagger out of town almost in a dance
I'd say was a waltz if the right music
were playing somewhere near enough to hear.
He lies down with cows nodding over him
as if to bless his tattered soul, I've heard,
and mumbles matins, while he sleeps, for them.

It's easy to blame wind for everything,
to imagine it's a drunk thief who leaves
clues we're supposed to be clever enough
to put together. But no wind asks us
for adoration. All wind insists on
is faith. And whatever music broken
men stagger home to, wind's there to lean on.
Still, even old men curse wind as they dance
in its arms as if it were memory
or something that forgives them everything.

75

Forgiveness is a sacred cow, I heard
him shout once in my sleep. Now, the cows have
wandered into town and wake me with prayers.
The lowing is a form of praise, I'm sure.
But are they praising the solace of sleep,
or is it the way the traffic light blinks
red and burns grief into their tired hearts
that will be cut out and sautéed and loved?
They pass through town like ghosts who are hungry
for the comfort and forgiveness of touch.

The wind can't forgive anyone. Nothing
is open late enough for light to bless
the heavy-hearted, lowing ghosts. I hear
a slurred voice shouting scripture at the cows.
Salvation's not easy, and all the pain
I know sleeps in bodies all over town
is clear in the drunk's voice and the chorus
of cows confused by a wind they followed
to a place where they watch themselves in dark
glass and low hymns that echo in my room.

When the drunk starts in shouting parables
from the New Testament, the ghostly cows
begin a chant I'm afraid might level
everything. And nothing can stop the drunk,
defrocked priest. This is his congregation
now, the bitter, lost souls he has to save
or die for. I want to sing some raw hymn
and have the gentle voices of the cows
harmonize and soothe the drunk's misery,
but it's been years and nothing comes to me.

So I go out and touch the cows that slip
through the sleeping streets because I don't know
what else there is to do, their lows rising
around me. Tired, I shiver and feel
blessed, stroking the soft hide of a Holstein.
In those eyes, I find the lost minaret
dancing, and recognize the suffering
its dance celebrates over stubborn fields
of corn that can only nod in a wind
I've heard tell of whose family name is Loss.

Or maybe not Loss at all, but something
closer to Forgiven. Translation is
always more or less an issue of faith.
The music I just make out moving with
the cows heading south of town makes me want
to serve up my own heart with a garnish
of sautéed onions and peppers. I don't
know where it's coming from, but the solemn
violins and cellos make my skin twitch
as if black flies bite and bite and won't stop.

I believe the music's the confession
of a lost minaret dancing through fields
where every crop is driven to witness
by the wind's arrogance. The bitter priest
has gone on ahead and left me with cows
who low what could be my name. Everything
I've lost hides in their enormous bodies,
and the odor of what could be whiskey
rises with their breath as if to forgive
the wind and bring back whatever's been lost.

from The Precarious Rhetoric of Angels

The hint of moraines on the horizon
argues against certainty. Unlike
the ruins of the shoe factory, where
it's said ghosts murmur and often cry,
barefoot and sore, glaciers are in it
for the long haul. Rust, though,
just hangs around and starts rumors
of couples laying blankets down
over ruins, touching each other
into moans. Not even sex
can disguise the flatness of a place
topographical maps turn gray
and the sky blurs, anonymous.
Any vague history of loss is oral.
Everything depends on the sad, moving tongue
and the safe lies of memory,
the past a ventriloquist, a mosque
gone gray surrounded by wheat. Autumn,
the fields on fire turning everything
to smoke, the mosque blurs into
a definition of what the heart gives up
to live in the flesh, a fervent prayer
faith makes things come back. It's said

glaciers will come south again
and erase scars from the last time.
That's just rumor. Nothing's certain
but the hacking of Sufis in the minarets,
smoke from their lungs
a kind of confession. It is
the world that's burning they love,
chants they cough through
elegies for everything consumed.
They don't know the history of ice and faith
and loss this landscape is
the text of. What they believe
is the world is formed by rusty voices
singing among ruins, that
any voice drifting with the ash of
the right crop can save everything,
that cars hurtling down the state route
are driven by dummies
they can throw their scarred voices into

and speak of sex and the anonymous sky.
Smoke can't hold up a mosque.
Local myths tell of feet pulled loose
by hooks in the river. It's said

the feet flatten wheat into what might be
topographical maps of distant countries
where the heart's had too much wine,
where ruins are stone and the ice
never reached. *The heart's a foreigner
everywhere*, a drunk says, faced
with a mosque in a field of wheat.
From the minarets, Sufis read maps
flattened in crops by wind or feet,
the sky a chant in the bitter language of rust
or fire thrown into the throats
of lovers moaning in the ruins of a factory.
Ash isn't all burning leaves.
Glaciers are breaking off, moving south
like ghosts of feet. It's said
when they get here history will buckle
under its guilt and religion
will lose its voice, gone hoarse
denying the world. For now,
farmers burn their fields to clear off
what hands can't, and Sufis
translate the smoke
into one of many voices, unheard.

THE MUSIC OF WHAT'S LEFT

The murmurous haunt of flies on summer eves.
—John Keats

Sad, to think of the murmurous haunt
of flies Keats spoke of
lost to the vagaries of genetics.

Not even the church—with its ash
and incense, its sin
and liturgies—can revive the lost song

of eighteenth century flies.
All stories told well
end in flies, or the flat murmur

of what isn't a heart but wind
in the architecture
of some cathedral burned,

sold, and renovated into a restaurant
where a man was murdered
who only wanted the Orange Roughy,

Cajun style. Ruin hums under
any ritual, and witnesses
disagree about the odd flash

one diner thought was evidence
of someone's birthday.
No one noticed the thin gauze

of dust drifting down from
what had once been
the cross-vault of a church set fire to

by a woman mad from the vagaries
of love. Now, the story,
once so clear-cut by lead bezels

into figures who would have cursed
the necessity of flies,
forgets itself, and the flies,

and focuses, sad, on how the bullet
sanctified the heart
it passed through. No fault of

its own, the coroner says later, drunk
and weary, into a mike.
This heart was sound, no sign

of a murmur or scar tissue. No damage
at all, except for
the cauterized tunnel. Bad design,

how knocking down one wall
compromises the whole structure,
leaves it unlivable, open to flies.

After the fact, witnesses,
and those not there, tend to talk
about warning signs. In this story,

they say the woman stared too cruel
at her fish. All the flies
since Keats hum the music

of what's left. Sad, how a face
can end up collapsed
on a fish, blackened. How old women

light candles in churches and listen
for the infinitesimal
hum of another world. Sad,

how choirs sing in the heat
and swat flies on Sundays,
the world insisting it is always

with us. *It wasn't the fish
that killed him, but love*,
the chef says. And the saints,

who saw it all, would nod
in their traps of lead and color,
if lead and glass could nod.

It's all about judgment. Sad,
to think it comes down
to the work of flies erasing the proof

bodies would leave. Sad,
how everyone danced ballroom style,
the woman taken out in handcuffs

ranting about cross-beams
and his heart, its
baroque architecture. Singing,

we slap each other's backs and laugh,
imagining elaborate tunnels
through which we might, one day,

escape, Keats' flies, nothing like
angels, come to show us, for
better or worse, the only way out.

THE BLURRED HAND HOLDS MORE

for Joanna

No doubt you've heard of the silo diver.
They say he times it
so the wheat bends south
in what wind there is
before falling in some semblance
of grace. No one can say
why he's never hurt. His skin,
pale, barely covers his veins
and glares over the wheat
that seems to reject him.
It's the direction of the wheat,
he says. It has to be
falling away. Not even wheat
breaks under him. His bones
should be a doctrine of desolate cracks
in the humming light
of the X-ray wall,
but they're as white and clear
as the Elvis painted
on the silo's side, a study in white
on white. It's the Vegas Elvis,
and the knuckles blur
where he clutches the mike,
as if the painter had to drink
in order to get it right,
and failed from too much bourbon.
It's a delicate balance.
So is his body and the wheat.
Any mistake and it's over.
Elvis didn't sing from his throat.
The voice came up coughing and raw
from being held under
the foul surface of the Tennessee swamp
that was all he had left
to call a heart in Vegas.
The silo diver whispers *Love me tender*
as he falls toward the wheat.
Maybe wheat can listen,
or maybe wind loves his bright body
falling through it, a song.
Locals say the Elvis of the silo

86

saves him, believing
the blurred hand holds more than a mike.
Tomorrow a crowd will gather
for his dive, the sky as gray
as Ohio gets. The diver's sore heart
will forget the wheat.
He'll dive for a woman
behind the fanatics who swear Jesus
smiles in blurred knuckles.
Not even Elvis will save him this time.

The sheriff tells the press the body shows no signs
of abuse, and the sweet scent she gives off isn't
explainable. A mute shepherd found the girl naked in bushes

and ran into town signing, his hands stuttering down
Main. Tonight, while the mute shepherd gets drunk,
the sheriff notices the sweet scent the girl gives off

seeps all over town. Tomorrow, his wife complains
at her deli about his hands, how, when he touched her
last night, she couldn't feel them. She tells a regular

where he touched her her body went numb. She wraps
the salmon and says it must be the girl, that sweetness.
It's unnatural, she says, *and getting worse.* The girl's

sweet-smelling body ignores them all. Someone sees
the sheriff walking down a back street, his hands
a blur in the dark, almost an unfinished notion

of hands. *The whole town stinks of her sweetness,*
the bartender tells the mute shepherd, making another
rum and Coke. Down the bar, a deaf woman is drunk,

her signing garbled, incoherent. The mute shepherd
can't make out a thing. The sheriff's wife closes the deli
and walks to the edge of town, to the quarry where

her last customer said she had seen her husband, sitting
on a rock, singing what sounded, from a safe distance,
like hymns. Out here, the sweetness is almost bearable.

She's surprised at first by the sheep milling about, crying,
but then remembers the rumors of the drunk shepherd,
the one who found the girl. The sheep must be looking for

him. From where she is she can see what's left of her
husband's hands moving as if he were giving directions.
But what his almost-hands sign in the air over the sheep

is not a map of the town, not the way to get to the bar where
the mute shepherd helps the deaf drunk out the door.
It's her body he signs to the abandoned sheep. She has

never been so uncertain what sweetness is. Her husband
reproduces every curve and imperfection of her body,
every subtle inflection. It is the most amazing thing

she has seen, her body drawn so sweetly by the blurs of
her husband's hands. The sheep head into town. Already
she hears doors slamming as people come out to see what is

happening, the bitter smell of the sheep cleansing the town
of the girl's unbearable sweetness. The sheriff is crying.
His wife goes to him and places his hands, which are hands

again, on her body. The shepherd leads the sheep out of town
and sings songs about women and pain and forgiveness.
No one is left awake to hear him and marvel. The sweetness

dissipates until only the girl smells so sweet. *It's not for
the living*, the bartender says to the deaf drunk at the end
of the bar again, *that sweetness. It's more than we can bear.*

The deaf drunk takes another drink and winks at the bartender.
Though she's never heard a word he's said, his voice
trembles across her flesh, the touch a sweetness she needs.

Dream a sad river, if you have to. Dream
a plain white sign with lines and numbers
to show how far the river's forgotten
itself. Make the river the Maumee. Say
it's low from drought, and poison. Drink it
in the diner's coffee just off the highway
where the waitress is friendly but tired,
her second shift in a row. She slips out of
her shoes without shame when you offer to
rub her feet for a meal. Not even this

could forgive how I walked with a woman
across the Maumee on rocks that longed
for any current, how we laughed standing
where the river had been, a long drought
letting us stand there and laugh. I could
rub the sore feet of every waitress
in every faded diner the length of this river
and only scratch my penance. Even lips
to calloused flesh wouldn't be enough. Being
tender is a beginning, with no end

in sight. I caressed a sad woman once
in the absence of a river, wanting
only to know the various textures
of flesh, my fingers tributaries of
a river I'm still learning is more fragile
than any raw water of fish and force
that swells and disappears with weather.
Touching a woman is the closest I'll come
to any kind of forgiveness. *Not enough*,
the recovered Maumee chants when I drive

the state route that follows it with a longing
a bruised waitress, her feet going numb
in a man's hands, could explain. If she could
remember a man with dust for hands
who touched her body until *it* was dust
and a car going by on the broken road,
close enough to be more than sound, lifted her
in its wake, I'd believe the past
has nothing to do with dust or rivers.
That it's a weathered sign remembering

a building burned down where people once ate
in the center of town, two charred bodies
found embracing in the ruin of ash
and smoke. Everyone recognized Rachel,
the woman who'd worked there so long
her name was coffee in the bitter mouth
of every lonely man in town. No one
could say why it was her shoes were off,
or who the man holding her was. The sign
leaves him nameless, a ghost seen on nights

the Maumee threatens to rise with the moon and moan
through the streets, erasing names. The woman
I touched on the raw bones of that river
had many names. I only knew one. Her ghost
moans beside me down streets missing
their signs. On one, she gets up to feed her baby,
a man snoring his side of the bed to
some other town down river that mutters
curses at any lovers who lie and touch
in grasses thick along its body. Maybe

what moves through her into the child
is the sad river her husband dreams.
Maybe no matter how many times
she forgets herself, or returns to the lover
who longs to rub her feet of all soreness
and doubt, it's this river she needs
to pray to, to pray for, to ask weather
to keep it from rising, or forgetting itself.
And maybe any longing is a dust
only a river swollen by weather

can wash off. Maybe all her names are prayers,
the faded white sign enough to forgive her
everything. Any river knows not to
lug a thing like guilt all the way to a gulf.
No matter how many names a river
picks up its length, it hums only one.
Until you break down and hold a river
all night, any name is just an excuse
for bitterness. To forgive yourself,
love every waitress and learn the foot.

DANCING IN MIAMI, OKLAHOMA

Old folks here say the sky
is a note held on a fiddle
longer than humanly possible.
They say they breathe bluegrass
in their sleep, a music
that makes the sky waver.
They have seen it tremble,
they say, and heard rain
hum melodies they swear they know

but can't name. One
old woman dances in
a frayed cotton gown every night
through the city park and home.
Boys grow up with the legend
of her withered flesh. Grandfathers
play old records at night
and swear her body once made
all of Oklahoma want

the sun to blind them just after
she left their sight. Fathers say
the one man who touched her
lives mad in a shack
alone at the edge of town,
where strays scrounge for scraps
and whimper at a sky
still out of whack
with the fiddle's music. Boys

throw rocks at the strays
and make fun of the lunatic
in the shack. History is
as much what people say
as what they do, and Oklahoma
is no more ground down
than any state. Dancers
under its callous sky
wouldn't be out of place flickering

across the tattered screen
in the theatre someone's been

restoring as long as the fathers
can remember. No one knows
what it was to begin with.
Teenagers drink and tell jokes
about the town's curves,
how the mayor's blocked efforts
to straighten Main. In his yard,

he watches an old woman dance
around the town's bend to a record
he breaks every night and buys
every day. His wife painted
baroque angels on the cornices
of the theatre and left.
Music can't restore anything
we lose. Grandfathers
can't swear to it, but believe

the old woman once played an angel
in a film where she restored a man
to his life. A Texas waltz
by Bob Wills helped her
into a gray sky at the end
of the movie. Everyone but the woman
goes to auctions. The rusted
farm equipment was theirs,
before the farms failed. No one

buys anything, but the auctioneer's voice
is a music of possibility
they want to believe. They want
to believe distance isn't everything,
and the rumor of touch
is enough to make strays forget
the note of the sky, enough
to bring gilded angels down
to save women who fall or dance

out of memories of falling.
Nothing, the mayor swears,
is actually straight. Everything is
at least a bit off. Old folks
don't care enough to argue.
They shut themselves in with old records
and whiskey to wait for

the lonesome night,
and a dancer they can count on.

HYMNS NOT ONE OF US WOULD RISK

In northern Ohio, false pear trees hum like sleep,
swarms of bees between the almost-blossoms.
To walk under the deceptive trees, humming,
is like waking from walking in your sleep
on the whitewashed porch of a woman
who hummed when you made love, knowing
she's inside, in bed with another man, asleep.
Some escapes are bargains. Others blossom sore
within us no matter the season. In Oklahoma,
though, they say the sky is indifferent,
and loss hums its way into actual fruit and dies.

Rituals don't always lead to salvation. It seems,
though, something always has to die. A god,
say, or the heart of a man at least. Or Wild
Willy's, closed for years and boarded up,
spray-painted by drunk teens humming what hurt
their suddenly anonymous flesh. Figures
they sprayed crudely are exaggerated. Love
isn't what they're about. Tonight, a drunk forgets
the bar's been closed years and bangs on the door,
the *Open* sign lopsided, and cries himself home.

Tonight, orchards just out of town are hymns
not one of us would want to risk, Ohio
full of state routes dotted with stands where fruit
is sold right out under the sky, nothing in it
but sweet absence. The drunks here are just
as forgetful, and stumble from bars humming
the same bluegrass. No one but a drunk
would sleep under false pear trees at the start
of summer, the trees humming down to him
of love. If bees, disturbed, drift down to sting him,
he'll wake with new pain and bless the dead.

The motel south of town houses drunk ghosts
who rant. All they think of is flesh,
and so loss. One remembers a woman
in love with nasturtiums, and wants
to touch the drunk flowers all over
a woman in the motel's bar, not tattoos
but memory. Don't forget, she told him,
how sad fucking can be. Don't forget
how you buried me in flowers once

and sweated over my body hours before
we watched, on TV, the local militia
give up and leave their compound,
confessing it had been a mistake,
the mistrust, their bodies bright with flowers
burned-in, one woman, naked,
a blistering field of nasturtiums.
The officer who covered her with a blanket
had scars on his hands that gleamed

in the harsh camera light, disguised
Morse code. Almost out of the picture,
a man sat in front of an open truck,
garish art on easels and jewelry
flashing bruised in a crude sun. Flowers
cheap plastic around him, the glass
he drank from was cartoonish. Maybe
memory is Morse code. *Dot:* music
in a motel room where bodies crack

and hum Elvis. *Dot:* cartoon animals
falling from clichés of Southwest rock
to flowers of dust, cringes of pure color.
Dot: ghosts stumbling through dust.
Dash: the pure hysteria of
a woman's body you believed
was prayer. *Dash:* the print of
a Japanese woman touching cloth,
quieting cynics with color. *Dash:* the calm

of flowers any lover could breathe in
without panic. *Dot:* the local militia
ranting dusty streets. *Dot:* a man

96

who hurls a woman against walls
for the clothes she wears. *Dot:* her
believing bruises are nasturtiums
blooming below her flesh. There is
no help. The options of memory
are not infinite, and cheap prints

in motel rooms are just lullabies.
The state route limps past town and curses
seasons the swamp rises. Ghosts
give up and forget flowers
and bourbon and loss. Love, she says,
hangs on motel walls tattooed, by headlights,
with the elongated forms of lovers.
Try to find, instead, a reproduction
of Utamaro's *Sewing.* Imagine

the woman's arms are nasturtiums
through the bruise of cloth,
the line she sights between her hands
the horizon. This is just
the left panel of an obscure triptych,
the woman's face a vague curse
of perfection. No motel room contains
Utamaro. The heart has to
live with being disappointed, or leave

for classier digs, for memory. The flowers
that cringe on her kimono
are nasturtiums. Furious, they incite militias
to burn themselves with flowers.
Bourbon, she said, tastes like a field
gone to bitter blossoms, the dead
left with dust and stale language. No ghost
is sober enough to argue. With memory,
nothing's set in stone. No one could

mistake the garish colors of a room
in this motel for a print by Utamaro,
where color is the pain he felt
for the loss of love in its object.
Break out the bourbon, she said.
The problem is we aren't nasturtiums,
and when we come back
we come back different. Try
naming every flower tattooed on

that woman in the bar who can't
remember her skin without color,
or which flower was first. No one
can get a thing out of the dead.
Across town tonight, she breathes
the furious scent of her husband's sweat
and comes. Garish art
can't make nasturtiums love,
or burn the heart into any flesh

with enough color to keep it from being
erased. To touch a tattooed lover
with Elvis singing low
is to mistake memory for the truth,
clichéd flowers for the longing
of the body. Nothing could be
more wrong. The code you believe
you've broken is too sad
and riddled with options to believe.

Succulents can break the heart in deserts,
the way the man roped to an elm and burned
would have said he left his body
tied to that burning. No one remembers
what he'd done. For some, such haloed figures
wailing in the distance are mirages,
signs of decaying angels who feed soil
and make their strawberries bitter.
That the man didn't die was a miracle.
Men who were there swear the flames just

went out, the charred flesh left with words,
a tortured syntax that made their ribs brittle.
Judgment, they say, sometimes comes in flames,
with signs sure enough to be read in flesh.
That man no one has the heart to touch, that fire
wouldn't have, whose tongue was seared dumb,
still growls at women, his charred mouth burning,
a language of longing and empty rhetoric.
The women have learned the vocabulary of
his grunts, and blush for past sins and dream

a blackened tongue turning their flesh to ash.
The women know the tongues of angels
are often dark. Angels know women sleep
between Heaven and The Fall. They swear
the voice they hear in dark bedrooms lit
only by the light of their translucent bodies
is God's. The man's lit flesh was a feeble light.
It was no one's fault, the mistake, and everyone's,
hate a bitter ash that drifts in the air
of ruined cathedrals that sing with wind. Maybe

it was the rope they bound him with that saved him,
words the men believed they saw on his body
the rope's last will and testament,
the rhetoric of the martyr. Sacrifice is
a mirage the heart would drink sand from and love
how its thirst was sated. What we believe
is almost never right, meaning too precarious
to depend on. The stone saints who'd tell us,
if they could, how wind burns their faces
have had their scars removed. The stone-cutter

99

pulled any arrows out and bound the wounds
and balanced the bodies on platforms
between the origin of praise and its objects.
Women are in love with the stone mouths
of saints. They imagine when the saints pray
they pray in the language of the jade.
They want their own prayers to live as long
without faith as it does without water.
Under the saints, they want to believe
there's enough water in the world to put out

everything that burns, to believe any soil
can produce strawberries sweet enough to heal
the most ashen mouth. The men who burned
the skin of the man made mute cower from
saints and the rhetoric of accusation. And jade
thrives even where soil's broken down,
a bitter garden, its color almost a dirge
in this town where guilt's an art people burn
into skin with colors that could be mixed
from ash. Elms lean toward town and implicate

everyone. Women cook elaborate meals
and leave them on the porch of the burned man
where something needs to be chanted fervent enough
to heal mottled flesh. Ribs are his favorite,
and the women make them so tender
stone tongues would shatter to praise them.
Strawberries they leave are never bitter. Miracles
can blind us enough to make us mistake
the heart for a comma in the grammar
angels use in cathedrals where the fallen

moan and hum the music of guilt. Envious
saints are just mirages of flesh in marble
or granite scarred enough. And angels praise
or extinguish flames, depending on their mood.
Not even saints guess right every time.
They enter deserts and speak to worn rocks
as if speaking to bones. Jade keeps them alive,
the water stored up in thick leaves. Carved
for cathedrals, the jade covers their feet,
a stone lie of succulents that break off,

too delicate a detail for weather to ignore.
Bitter rain, leaning south with cold,
is a scalpel. So much nonsense has been written
to define what's lost. Language can't
restore stone or glass or light. Not even angels
can speak words that could heal the flesh
of the man burned to an elm. His throat,
the women say, swirls with a smoke he coughs
drunk and stumbling through town, the music
of his charred lungs an accompaniment

for the dim, fluorescent hum of street lamps.
They believe stars are bodies that have
become burning, the tongues they speak in
precarious and orchestrated to confuse
a man's love for a woman with some myth
large enough for the sky. Saints have
to suffer in stone for a charred, broken man,
forgiveness a faint detail almost hidden
behind the hands of a saint reaching for
what could be strawberries, or bitter hearts

strung on a vine and pinned to an arbor.
The stone lattice could almost be the words
of a prayer in a language the angels
can't decipher, the stone-cutter's secret
praise for the woman he loved. So much
is easily burned in this world. Even cold
can burn flesh, or cringe jade leaves
into scarred and brittle tongues with nothing
to say about saints or lovers. And angels
long to enter women and burn themselves

into a seared language not even God
would understand, his memory of being
a man faded by now, his suffering
as dim as the sand dunes in a desert
lit by a quarter moon that could slice
stone berries like a sickle. North of town,
in an old cathedral opened by fire
to the wind and rain, a scarred man hums
in the rotting pews, his music rising
out of bitterness, blessing everyone.

from Open Between Us

HOUSE ON POPLAR STREET

All forms that perish other forms supply.
—Alexander Pope

Patterns
The interstate came through and buried it.
Faith was easier, living in one place.
There are photographs of the house

where I learned things struggle to remain,
ghostly buds blooming on the near-dead oak
whose gnarled roots broke the backyard

where I buried pets I haven't thought of
for years. All of us seek the comfort
of talking to the dead in some form.

Carvings on rock and bone whisper
in glass cases in museums
everywhere. Place is its own history.

I'd have to carve runes into the road
to be clarified by headlights.
This used to be open land. The corpses

of animals mark off the distances,
the long patterns of living
hard to break. Memories lead back to

actual places. The ache of what's not
left forces these lines into
a form where ghosts come to rest.

Belief
Surfaces I knew by touch are missing.
In landscapes where ghosts
say words that comforted them

alive, I pass ruins and count the miles,
saying the names of towns
where it's possible to find more

than the lonely figures of local spires.
The faith that keeps people fixing
what breaks can be found in towns

named by dull white signs. What I broke
in the house on Poplar Street
can't be fixed, and though I want to

believe in the names I carved
with butter knives
in painted wood, belief isn't enough.

This elegy can't summon back anything
that could ever speak.
What we touch of what we love is mute.

Names
Form is the passion for return, but this
can only come back
to a place no longer real,

where an oak stood that continued,
in the death cracking its heart,
to feed pale blooms that broke each year

from its scarred limbs. This was faith,
the struggle to keep providing.
Ghosts that wander between towns

with words they've loved can name
the places they are forgetting.
From us they want the names of

what we've touched. I want what I know
to be enough to satisfy the ghosts
who speak names they can't

bear to forget, like *poplar.* I want to be
able to pass on through them,
the familiar all I need to sustain me.

THE UNSPEAKABLE

Moist wind off the lake
can lift us
out of any sense

of direction. Gulls drift between
signs of life
in an overcast sky.

Those of us at home wait
for rain, the light
unbelievable. Imagine air

with the tone of a black and white
TV screen at night,
the breath of someone asleep

in the next room. There's no drama
not human, yet
this sky, laden with

its clouded light, seems tragic.
The rain's a relief,
letting everyone share

what unspeakable light soaks
the world. I imagine
rain touching windows,

fogged-over and streaked,
you speaking
with people who are mysteries

when you're here with me,
when we ask
one another to please

pass one thing or another
and furtive glances
of flesh force us to

imagine distances. Today the sky
is more important
than anything I can't find

words for. A single gull
sails the wind
and this loved world

shivers with a grief-stricken light
so absolute
it could stun

any one of us who happened
to look up
from our work.

THE WORST WE CAN DO

No one would put me in a poem, he said.
Waiters in French cafés are everywhere,
but not me. We were sharing a last drink

in a Midwest bar. He could've been
anyone's father but mine.
I always knew when my father got home.

The door would slam. No matter how
drunk, he never forgot to lock it.
Nights he got home early, he'd fall asleep

half-naked in front of the TV which droned
until my mother got out of bed
to turn it off. Sometimes she left him

there, limp in his wrinkled clothes.
Other nights she'd say his name
until he got up and followed her to bed.

It hurt her, and I couldn't understand how
she could limp through such pain
and still love him. But she did.

The man who would pour me a free one
at the end of the night, who was not
my father, once told me, *A good woman is*

what this place needs. We finished our drinks
and went home. I wish I had
told him love makes it through the worst

we can do to it, but I didn't see that till now.
And by now it would do him no good.
Either it would be old news, or unbelievable.

Rain again. My wife wants to listen
with the lights out. This means
we can't make the lake, she says.

Or afford the faith it would take to
leap naked over a fire we'd built

on the darkest day of the year and believe
we called back the sun.

Days we do make the lake, gulls are hungry
and circle, assuming
we've come with bread to fill the air.

Across the courtyard a light comes on,
disrupting the dark. Imagine,

my wife says, hillsides lit up
in winter with prayers set
by men and women to call back the sun.

There's an island nearby we like
to visit, walking slow,
trying to name the voices of birds,

warblers singing. All of human history
hasn't made anything better.

My wife sings to sparrows, and laughs
on bridges barn swallows nest under.
They skim water without touching the surface.

We can't help but love their certainty.
My wife, made unsure by weather,
sings in Welsh. It goes well with the rain.

It could be a song about fires on hillsides
where families chanted prayers
they'd been taught, believing

what they did made a difference. Maybe
it did. Sometimes I'm not sure

~

how real something needs to be
before it's believable.

My wife wants to know if the lake's possible
tonight, after the rain. I think

of the surface marked with rough weather.
Yes, I want to tell her. I tell her *Yes*.

There's no reason my wife should believe
how the light of this storm
folds into the backyard walnut trees.

Maybe she doesn't want to see what light does
to this world she's denying. She talks of

a woman who disappeared into
lush desert, her body
found, dried out, days later.

Her footprints were not, she says, frantic
periods, but calm ellipses.

It's difficult to go on from here,
to remember she's in
the lobby of a clinic in the Southwest,

surrounded by women who seem no more
than excuses for suffering.

I want her body to hold more, to believe
the light they pass over her
can turn back enough darkness.

The storm has broken here. No light
left to speak of. She reads
stories from the local paper. Tonight

it's about a man in Minnesota
whose son didn't call
on Father's Day. She reads of the blood

washed off walls in the son's house,
the bodies carted out, and wishes
they had interviewed the father.

She wants to know, she says,
what it's like to kill someone so close.

I want to ask if she can imagine
what it's like to be so forgotten,
but can't be sure how she'd answer.

112

~

The dark cells in her body are quieter,
she says. She feels better,
but says no when I ask to visit.

She's not ready. She folds out
the paper. Another story.
I want to erase them all. Just one

more, she says, and reads of
a man in a wheelchair
who saved a baby from drowning

in a backyard pool. It's almost enough
to make me believe the dark
is dying inside her. A black branch

has broken and fallen against our home,
scraping brick as wind gives it life.

There's so much I want to say.
Where she is the stars are
out in unselfish numbers. Across

the damp courtyard, a light comes on.
It's good to know this world
isn't empty, that people are

coming together in rooms full of light,
a man and a woman forgetting
why they yelled this morning.

He's inside her and she's urging him on.
By morning this may be forgotten,
but tonight, for someone, being together

is a celebration, and enough. I want
to call back, to tell her I want her home,

despite the storm. I want to live with
the hard evidence of her going.

We said little not suggested by the map
kept open between. You knew stories
of places I'd never heard of. When you didn't,

we made up local histories and lied
about legends. We made love in
every state we passed through. Near towns

that showed on the map, you turned the radio on
for human voices. We kept to state routes
to avoid traffic and cut through towns

we didn't see a soul in, this country emptier
than I knew. You were quick to point to
the signs of people—house lights slanting over

flat land we both knew was too open. For
everyone who lived in those lit rooms,
the only salvation was the brief time of touch

after days of working on things they didn't get.
Like the man swallowed by the raised hood of
the same Ford pickup in every town. We came to

expect him and feel better when we saw him,
stripped to the waist and dark with engine grease.
We waved and in each town he waved back.

Sometimes a woman came out of a house in need
of a paint job to bring him a sweating can
of beer. In some towns, there was only the house

and the need. Sometimes a child would be in
the cab pretending to drive. Other times,
no one around for miles, we wanted to stop

and have a beer with him, say how good it was
to see him again, how worried we were
about him being alone. He'd have talked of men

he knew by their first names who welcomed him
at the local tavern, men intimate with
the hard taste of wind who had taken home

the ruin of their lives when they were younger
and less tired. We're tired, too,
you'd have said. He'd have looked us over

and laughed. Stay out here long enough,
he'd have said, and you will be. I would have
thanked him for the beer, and we'd have climbed

back into our truck and driven as far as we could
before stopping to make love in a different state
no matter how tired we were. In the next town,

the Ford would've been by the road, the hood
raised as if he'd just gone inside. You would
have said he wasn't alone, that he'd gone in

to hold a woman whose lips were full of
local color that could pull us out of the stories
we made up to pass the time between towns

close enough to send the music that led us
to this northern city where the air
is wet and failure has signs other than dust.

Against all good sense, I want to go back
to one of the towns he was alone in
and invite him to the tavern for a drink.

He'd open up, admit his failures, and everything
lost to the stubborn silence of
the wrecked engine would be recovered.

We'd know each other by our first names,
which would be the same, and after
a long afternoon of pool and drinking

we'd step out and, light-stunned, not be able
to say which of us should stay in town
and which should start the drive back to you.

We wouldn't care who stayed and who left,
only that whoever stayed would be able to
make the engine in that Ford turn over.

from A Short Bestiary of Love and Madness

In a coastal village on the southern tip of Italy,
an old man makes ocarinas.
Everyone knows his work.

They can hear someone playing a slow ballad
blocks away, it can be night
and, full of sorrow and wine, still

they know someone's playing a Mantegna.
No one knows why his ocarinas
make a music that lingers like an ache,

but they know this allows them to love
more than they could without it.

No one knows Mantegna makes his ocarinas
from the bodies of needlefish who swim
into a net hung over the side of his rowboat.

No one has heard what Mantegna's heard.

One day, cooling himself, head under the water,
he heard a needlefish sing to its lover,
a sound so beautiful he nearly drowned listening.

So he caught a needlefish and used it
to make his first ocarina,

and when he blew the first note he knew
the sorrow and passion of the needlefish
lived in what he had made of the body.

No one knows his sorrow. The needlefish
swim into his net, closemouthed,
giving up their bodies for his art,

but they won't sing for Mantegna, who cries,
caressing fish bodies into music.

If a cardinal communes with bare trees,
blessing each in turn,

the arc of his passage through cold air lingers,
a frail admonition against forgetting,

or a taut line on which to hang
something delicate enough to heal despair.

And if memory is a red bird's erratic flight among pines,
a lover's voice can call a cardinal out of the ribs,

and something like a song can tremble the body.
And if pines can ache from the cardinal's absence,

cold air can hold the breath of lovers
long enough to let a cardinal pass through it

and pull it into a form which could be
a prophecy or a curse. And if

the cardinal's a sacred bird blessing the world,
the song is a lover's name, over and over,

rising lyrical out of a small red body,
burning the world clean of all sin, all despair.

There's a tropical country where the people have such brilliant dreams no one gets enough sleep. They keep waking, often trembling, sweating in their sheets, other times trying to catch their breath, occasionally smiling. They've forgotten the name of their country, though every night hundreds wake with one of the syllables of the forgotten name on their tongues. Sometimes an entire family comes awake at just the right times—each with a different syllable of the name in their mouths—if they were all in the same room and listened to the sounds they whispered they would hear their country's name hanging in the air between them like someone's idea of paradise. Memory, though, isn't alone in being affected by this lack of sustained sleep. Something wonderful happens in that country due to the ferocity of dreams. Every now and then, someone has a thought that becomes real. The macaw, for example, didn't exist until a small boy, waking from a savage and colorful dream, remembered the bird. That morning there were macaws in every *macauba* in the boy's village, breaking open the fruit of the palm trees with their remarkable bills and calling to one another with voices that had to have been dreamed to be real. The people in this country without a name have a saying, that the world will continue until the night a woman wakes with the true name of the moon passing over her lips. The name, whispered by the waking woman, will call the moon down, the saying goes, and the oceans will rise to cover the land, to embrace both the earth and the moon, and everyone will drown with the word for *love* in some forgotten language on their lips.

The sea urchin, full of urges, huddles
in its limy shell which grows
thick with the scratched residue of desires

the urchin won't even whisper. People used to
believe the future could be read
on the opened shell of a sea urchin.

Predictions were made based on scrawls there,
and sometimes, because the world is
unpredictable, it seemed they came to pass.

Everything's percentages. What was written
on the urchin's shell was never the future,
just the recording of unspoken urges

and a fevered attempt to find a language
to speak something into being.
But the sea urchin is pierced by spikes

that keep all possibilities at bay,
those which might harm it
as well as those which might lead to joy.

The sea urchin scribbles on its shell and drifts,
sad, in the ocean, alone,
speared by the awkwardness of its form.

The sand grouse was once a god. Like most gods,
the sand grouse never asked for the honor.

The artists of a nomadic tribe carved sandstone
replicas for altars the strongest carried on their backs.

Carved sand grouses still roost, buried in deserts.
Sometimes a simoom uncovers a stone bird

and descendants of the nomads dream of the sand
grouse. This god who never asked to be

a god speaks to the sleepers about love,
the grainy madness that buries the heart

made of stone. The sand grouse speaks
of passion in the tongues of dream-birds.

When the dreamers wake, they hold one another
as though they believe the body they hold

could be an illusion carved out of soft rock,
a figure of what could be divine.

Touch is redefined each time dolphins make love. The smooth bodies swim for miles together, twirling through water, a dream of what ballet could be without the awkwardness of the human form in gravity, and the water whispers stories that calm each body that swims or floats through it. Even sharks forget their hunger. Because dolphins sacrifice their sleek bodies to passion, sharks do a dance in the dark water that could be mistaken for regret, or the longing for sorrow to cling to them like remora. When they rise into water changed by light, where passion becomes sound, the bodies of sharks hum a music that's a kind of touch. It's from such moments the stories come, of sharks brushing past the legs of human swimmers. Dolphins spin through water, joined to one another and to the music that touches even the awkward forms of men and women who will tell the story for years of how it must have been a kind of grace that kept the sharks from attacking. Of how warm their bodies were. How gentle the touch.

OF TOUCH AND VOICE AND OTHER PLEASURES

Grass and twigs and flashes of color,
woven together and seen from the right distance,

can speak of a passion that smolders
until breath passed from one mouth to another
resuscitates the flame and returns it

to the sky over a field whispering a story
about the male bowerbird which builds
boudoirs of grass and twigs and flowers

to call his mate back from a sky
that suffers the circle it makes of the world.

And the sentence this flame speaks,
just a gray wisp away from being
nothing, could be the song

the male bowerbird sings threading grass and twigs
to build a haven for his mate from
the debris of the world the sky circles.

The bowerbird flies through the sky's indifference
to gather the bits of what could be memory

he needs to build his bower, a temple
for an angel he believes in
without proof or any expectation of proof.

The passion of his weaving is just his nature.
The temple he builds won't house an angel
or call anything out of the sky but sorrow.

Or maybe an angel *is* called out of the sky by the patterns
the bowerbird weaves that reminds her of touch
and voice and other pleasures of being in the world.

Maybe she comes down to the world
and the bower and the bird waiting beside it
with only his passion and his faith.

And after she's touched the bird into a pleasure
even the circuitous sky longs for,

~

maybe she leaves him alone again with what was
never more than grass and twigs and dying flowers.

Maybe she leaves him the memory of a passion
he'll try to sing the rest of his life
without so much as a prayer of getting it right.

THE LIME AND DUST OF DISGUISES

The hawksbill's carapace is no cathedral.
Though the vault the bone rises into
is enough to hold as many lies,

it has no stories of saints in stained glass
to filter light onto the body
that must bear its weight. There's no altar

other than the body, and no myth
of a god impaled on driftwood

to make the hawksbill feel a guilt large enough
to separate it from the shell men and women covet.

The hawksbill swims warm, blue waters
and doesn't worry about sin
or the conventions of saints or martyrs.

It doesn't worry about tales of water turned into wine,
the lame flying, or the blind learning
languages the lost mutter in their curled sleep.

The hawksbill doesn't worry about parables
that would evaporate the oceans

so men and woman could walk the bones
of forgotten fish
and find the buried ramblings of their own hearts.

It doesn't worry about revelations that speak of
how, at the end, shellfish will swallow
the lime and dust of their disguises and dance

naked in the vapor. The hawksbill only worries
about the vanity of men and women,

how its carapace can be carved into objects
they use to preen and pass themselves off

as adorned. The hawksbill dreams of finding
a crude but elegant figure painted in
primitive colors on the scorched walls of its carapace,

~

a figure that holds in its elongated, awkward arms
the body stripped of its shell.

The hawksbill wants the body in that painting
to be a symbol for its soul.

And high up in the rafters of its carapace
it wants the figure of a lover to have been drawn,

rough, crouching, touching what could be
its body or, in the right light, love.

Mantas fly the shallow waters of the ocean,
their wings swirling the bright water down

as if to send light into the depths—a blessing
for fish who never rise far enough

for their bodies to glow, a prayer for grace
in the violent world. An old fisherman

likes to tell the story of when a manta got caught
in his net. He swears the story is true

and tells it for drinks in the local tavern.
We who have heard the story before

shake our heads each time he begins, but
we listen, secretly wanting to believe

that, when the old man reached down
and touched the manta's skin,

a song entered through his fingers. We want
to believe this is what he strums

on his Spanish guitar as he tells the story.
It's the song we pay for with drinks.

That, and the pleasure we find in believing
it was the manta's love that saved it,

convincing the old man to cut the net and let it glide off.
Saved by love. To believe this, we'd pay anything.

And we do. Night after night. All our lives.

from Structures the Wind Sings Through: A Poem

This song that begins in the heart erupts
from the throat into voice, and voice, uttered,

becomes everything. The landscape wants to
insist on being-for-its-own-sake, but

we know such arguments are false. Maybe
no one's left who can speak of this road

the way it was when it was first put down.
What signs were posted, no one can say.

The past gives in to insects and the dust of
anonymous construction that must have

just finished, the dust still visible, doing
some obscure waltz in the air, almost

music made physical. The dust
turns the weary faces on placards—

how the missing looked when last seen—
vague and emblematic, a single person

gone missing not enough to shake language
out of its amnesia. Words require

continents sunk under waves to record loss.
Even then, it's not a question of

recovery but memory. The way fog,
dissipating, leaves damp patches

for a while. The sun, though, has always
advocated forgetting, to make room

for tomorrow. As if time were linear,
and finite. Time is just a revision

we make of things. It leaves wounds in
the landscape large enough to swallow

whole herds of buffalo. All the dances
the Sioux meant to call back and praise the sun

turned their own feet to dust,
in time. The dust that's a haze

in the skies of landscapes Turner painted
without ever having met a Sioux,

sparrows almost unrecognizable flickers
his stiff brush etched in the fog

of color that's the world in dissolve.
Faith often made it onto his canvases,

exotic animals bent to drink from pools
reflecting a surreal sky, camels

perhaps, or those buffalo just before
a sinkhole opens under them. Sometimes

there is only the land about to shiver
open. There are Turner mornings

even here, the water tower, in fog,
a tribal mask etched on this dim excuse

for a sky. What god would someone become
wearing this mask? Maybe the god

of trailer parks, twisted wind its sign
for expressing loss. This god is

a modern god, which means it doubts
its own existence and the possibility

of a faith that could revise the world
to make gods possible. The god of trailer parks

has read Einstein, and knows the limits
of linearity. The chicken and the egg

question, this god knows, was never more
than a distraction. The god of trailer parks

has argued this with road crews drunk in bars
where the light was thicker than Turner

would paint it. A kind of light that recalls
Caravaggio, and a jukebox full of

blues and classic country ballads. Smoke
loves slow, sad rhythms, the lyrics

familiar stories of abandon and loss. Always,
someone is broken enough to feed

quarters all night into the jukebox. Sorrow,
music claims, is better swallowed whole,

better when it covers everything left
or left out in the world, as if it were

the dust of some obscure construction.
Did Leopold, after making glass flowers

so real bees would die before giving up
trying to taste their pollen, have to

spend days wiping the almost invisible
glass dust off everything? What does it mean

if he missed some, a layer of glass
so fine it couldn't cut flesh but could

reflect light in ways we'd call music
if we were able to look long enough

to hear it? In Hopper's canvases,
light hums tunes we hum along with

if we study the paintings long enough.
Isn't this the music we would hear

if we went to the circus and sat close
to the center ring and gasped under

the frenzy of acrobats dangerous
in the smoky air of ropes? The truth is,

some music hums below every surface.
Even the surface of the fat man,

who sweats beside us on the sagging,
rented pew. Where his sleeves end

there's a cluster of trees tattooed, each leaf
a perfect work of art. The whole forest

shivers, as if in some tropical storm,
when the fat man struggles to breathe.

Asleep, he wheezes the thick music of
a calliope that starts the costumed elephants

dancing a dance the woman adorned in sequins
doesn't recognize. It could almost be

something out of Bosch. One sad elephant
shrugs off its costume and lies in the dirt

in a stance that seems familiar, though
we can't place it till a little girl yells

*It's the Sphinx. Look, Mommy, that elephant
is pretending to be the Sphinx.* And it is,

that's suddenly clear. The other elephants
dance around the one lying with its legs

straining out in front of it. Suddenly
the air is full, not only of the dust

kicked up by the musical, gray behemoths,
but also of sparrows, flickering in

perfect time with the pachyderms' dance.
The sequined woman has given up

and sits with the fat man, touching him,
the one she's never been able to

stop loving. She strokes the expanse of
his torso, and the music coming from

his grotesque body is beautiful enough
to reconcile all of us to the sorrow

that waits outside this tent. Each of us
will leave this dusty womb of music

and grace soon enough. For now, elephants
dance with the sparrows and acrobats

float over us, figures Dürer might have etched
behind the suddenly *almost* naked bodies

of Adam and Eve, and each of us rises
to embrace the man or woman or child

we came with. Humming a song we feel
in our chests, we all begin to dance.

from Monks Beginning to Waltz

My father says they prove grace is possible
even in this world,

that memories only need the occasional
slow drag of wings to stay aloft.

Once he said they were the land itself,
its desire to dip and rise

into rumors of topography. They drift
thermals off flat tar, dark angels

some Italian might paint. I've seen them pray
over a deer with a second skin of flies,

an altar panel Tiepolo would not have
placed behind the crucifix. Angels

often carry us to suffering. My father's
breath when he stumbled home

some nights smelled like loss. In my room,
light casting shadows of his hands

on the wall, he'd open our private aviary.
Grace, he'd whisper, his hands

settled into their slow, drifting forms,
is what keeps us from giving up.

Cancer has left his hands topographical maps
of pain. He lies about

remission, saying faith heals most
anything, and speaks of

some church in Italy his company hid out in
one night. A local told him

Tiepolo painted the frescoes that flickered
around them. Explosions

141

brought the stained glass to life.
In the tortured light of saints

they cowered in the rafters. *Could've been
the end of the world for all*

they knew, he says. The wounded
were so afraid my father and a friend

opened fire. The first hit hung there,
claws stuck in wood.

It fell later, in the silence after
the shelling. They had to

shoot the rest out of the air. *It was
awful*, he says. Trapped

by the amnesia of panic, they flapped
from stained glass to wood,

looking for the rip artillery had left in the roof
where they had come in.

One finally broke through the flickering image
of Saint Francis and died.

Two escaped through the shattered monk.
My father knelt in that church

for forgiveness, without knowing who it was
he was asking. *It could have been*

God, he says, *or all the dead and dying.*
He wants to say it was

the two who got out, angels who flew
through Francis into a sky,

broken, with room for grace. He says
those blessed birds still drift

adagios to hymns only the dead can hear,
a music he swears is forgiveness,

the way he swears sorrow is something
no angel could ever consume.

THE PASSION OF RADISHES

Tonight the moon's a bitter radish. A man tastes
its memory on his tongue and thinks of a woman
he hasn't touched in years. The radish moon

murmurs overhead, its red light stretched over
the hard white heart of the man's remembering

a night he brought her fingers to his lips
just after she'd sliced radishes for a salad,
her skin, touched with the bitter juice,

a delicacy. That night, when they made love,
the radishes mingled with the scent of her flesh
and his heart burned a white he could never

tell her. Tonight, he feels the hard, white center
of everything the light touches and wants to

go out and buy some radishes, to slice them
so the red light from the radish moon
sinks into the exposed flesh, and the scent

of the opened radishes rises to give memory
a body he can hold, soft fingers he can raise
to his lips and kiss with the passion of radishes.

He wants to slice the moon and place its light
over a woman asleep beside another man.

He wants the radish light to be a memory
that lets her smile in her sleep and start to hum.

The woman in your bed cuts a pear in halves
that could be hands, palms up to be read.

She says strings in the fruit tell the future.
This line, she says, *is guilt*. If the pear's

strings could be stroked, the music would
slice any heart that's hung too long

in gnarled trees. *This heart*, she whispers,
licking pear juice from your skin, *is wrinkled*.

No one would slice it. The heart is not
a fruit. Not even rumors of touch

can change that, not even the scent of
her back your fingers chant at night.

The heart slices touch across the palm's flesh.
It's there, the future. The trick is

to touch the lines like the strings of a violin
and not let the music suffer the history

of sorrow, a pear all bruise. The trick is
to believe each half remembers

the music in every branch, the song of
the flesh. The trick is to forget the pear.

The heart is not something to slice open.

THE BLESSING OF ONIONS

Last night you dreamt of onions,
their layers a curse.

At the heart of an onion even music is
a crying, the whole world blind.

You fumbled through the bulb and felt markings
on the curved walls, a language.

Somewhere a woman sang archaic hymns,
her voice peeling each lyric

down to grief. You wanted to be touched
in the tortured heart of the onion. You shivered

alone and blind in the onion which is
the heart of this rancid world

where no matter how many layers
we pull around us, our hearts

are still red and sore with feelings we'd slice
and sauté with mushrooms in butter.

The bland taste of the world this morning is
a curse only an onion could remove.

In some bar in Juneau the sky collapses,
stone drunk, in your arms and weeps.

Wolves press muzzles to the front window
with the stained-glass woman
you've imagined in your arms instead of the sky.

Her body's the map of an Alaska you wouldn't know
till you got her home and took her clothes off,

her skin whispering of the love wolves have
for everything the landscape holds. The sky is

still crying, your blouse soaked. An old man
with Jim Beam at the bar winks at your breasts.

The tundra is warm tonight, the sky whispers,
potted, from your lap. Whiskey

and sad music disguises the grain of wood
you read the future in. A woman will
go blind and touch her way alone across Alaska,

rumors of wolves whispering directions
in her cold ear while she dreams of
a town in Montana a man was murdered in.

His eyes could have brought any sky to
its knees. Birds too far off to be named

with certainty drifted in his near-vacant eyes
until the hole the bullet left filled up
with the longing of any wound for closure.

Back in the bar in Juneau, the sky confesses
any future you believe in
is a body in the first stages of decay.

The wolves drinking sour mash in Montana
are more gnarled, and confused.

They often end up lost, stumbling out of town
after downing all the whiskey they can bum.

147

~

A wind down from Alaska ruffles their fur
into maps that rename towns
and send tourists down wrong roads

where houses collapse into sinkholes from mines
no one bothered to warn anyone about.

No song can comfort the sky in Juneau tonight.
It's had too much cheap whiskey.

And the woman who lost her sight pets wolves
outside the bar. You whisper to the sky,
asleep in your lap, who mumbles something

about murder and love winking out
like the northern lights gone agoraphobic.

The eyes of a dead man in Montana remember
the blind face of a woman whose hands

were birds that drifted currents over his flesh.
The language of birds in any state is a blessing.

The sky will be hung over in the morning.
No woman, blind or not, can touch a whole state
and not come away with something more

than knowledge. You're sure of it. Even if
the sky is confused and drooling in your lap.

The wolves will stagger out of town and howl
a music to accompany sorrow.

And no map, not even the skin of a woman
who makes your hands blind,
can show you how to walk to Juneau

in winter. Ice and mountains and wrong
weather cut the town off on any map.

The wolves know ways down out of the mountains,
but air is how men and women come and go.

~

Whiskey rewrites street names. A blind woman
touches your face while the sky hallucinates
colors that pray and wink in and out

like some confession whispered from the next booth
by someone so drunk they think they are
in church and you could absolve their sins.

The hands of the blind woman look startled
in the variegated light coming from the woman
you've dreamed of on the window of this bar.

They could almost be birds that know which direction
to fly to love where they end up.

The sky will be jealous tomorrow. For now,
it can only mumble curses
into the wood left warm by your body

while the blind woman leads you out and places
your awkward hands on the wolves,

telling you how to touch them so their fur
forms a map you can follow home.

They put the animals down early.
The horses are flying by midnight.

The cows argue with Sartre. What about
the milk? they ask. Jean-Paul
pitches hay into the loft and doesn't answer.

By morning he'll be exhausted,
the white around his mouth a concession.

The loft will be full and the heat more
than anyone expected.
The hay will spontaneously burn

and take the most worn-out horses with it,
their wings turning to ash.

Others will escape, their bodies
haloed by smoke. People will run into

the barn on fire and come out carrying calves
or foals in blankets wet down and smoking.

For now, hay teases the moon and no one
thinks of flames. Not the horses,

playfully strafing the Pacific. Not the cows,
who have backed Wittgenstein into a corner

and are about to show him language isn't
necessary, or even real.

And not the men and women who make love
in dim rooms without language,
their bodies full of hay beginning to smoke.

The moon has finished its rounds and stopped in
the local tavern for a few whiskeys.

When it says it was the damnedest thing,
those horses flying like that,

~

no one is drunk enough to believe it,
or sober enough to recognize the moon.

In the barn, hay dreams of soil
that won't let it go. Smoke that will

fill the barn before the flash point tomorrow
is playing poker, bluffing everyone

into folding. The moon, drunk, stumbles down
dim streets where houses sink
two inches a year, shouting curses and raving

about horses burning in the air. Sartre,
sad with wine on a sinking porch,
wants to put an arm around the moon

and make it talk about a woman. He needs
to hear the moon say it is
always about a woman. He needs

the fog to lift and take the porch with it.
Everything must go, he says,

and wants to tell those damn cows
milk is an illusion and proves nothing.

He wonders what *can* be proven,
with the moon full of cheap whiskey.

They put the animals down early, and nothing
has gone right since. Wittgenstein,

born again, stands on a corner and shouts
at the moon, asking if it's been saved.

Hay mumbles an incoherent smoke in its sleep.
In one of the sinking houses,

a man turns over to look at the woman
sleeping beside him and thinks
she could be smoke. Her eyes closed

and galloping, she could be dreaming she is
flying on the back of a horse.

~

Or the moon could be kissing her breasts,
its drunken hands a reminiscence

of passion. Too much watered-down whiskey
means the moon can't finish this.

The house sinks a little more under
the sad weight of the moon collapsing

in the woman's dream. The idea of salvation,
Wittgenstein shouts at the moon's back,
cannot arrive. It has to have been there

from the beginning. The broken moon laughs.
It knows nothing is saved. Only

nothing. The rest, the moon whispers
to a woman asleep in a sinking house,
is already lost, was from the start.

Wittgenstein and Sartre know what it means
when horses burn in the sky
a drunk moon has forgotten. What love means

when you've got nothing and have to bluff.
What smoke means along a horse's flanks.

Passion can't be forgotten. It hovers
around the flesh. It's not enough,

the moon says, to believe love whispers
stories of air and the purity of flames
into the twitching ears of horses. Or

that love could convince the cows to stop arguing
and just listen to the world. They know

hay is restless in the barn, feeling tossed aside,
forgotten. The moon knows the damage

loss can lead to. Even now smoke is calling
for one last hand and grinning.

~

The moon has made it home and dreams
of a woman who could pull it down
and make it believe nothing suffers or drowns

in any water anywhere. Charred horses
trot the air over waves condemned
with litter, their hooves almost touching

all that's left of rotted barns and the porches
the moon hears, even asleep,

sinking in the world that sleeps and dreams
of the moon. Sartre curses at
the hay he finds everywhere. In his bed,

he writes a love letter on the warm belly
of a woman whose name he's afraid
to imagine, in a language he can't

pronounce. What she whispers, asleep,
could start hay smoking. And has.

And the cows curse any language
written on skin that's burning.

Wittgenstein drinks sacramental wine
and stutters his way through hymns
his mother sang to sober his father,

sprawled in grass, a crucifixion
which goes completely ignored.

Not even the moon is drunk enough
to do more than laugh

at the gesture, its light turning the grass
the soothing color of milk.

And the question of what is real
smokes under surfaces until
something catches and everything's flames.

153

RUMORS WHISPERED UNDER DARK ROBES

The kingdom of heaven is a condition of the heart
—Friedrich Nietzsche

The heart's a chapel where nuns pray
for the world they deny themselves.

The walls are delirious with crabs,
a Latin cross on every shell,

whose clicking infects the sleep of nuns
who dream of rosaries and cruel beaches,

the moon the baseball cap of an aching boy
the nuns would lock in the chapel

when he said words they couldn't bear.
Crabs reached for him and his heart

would pull its Mariners' cap down
and start to chatter a crazed rosary

in to a boy at bat who'd never hit a single
ball even close to out of the infield.

Crabs he cracked the shells of on beaches
were obstinate hearts tired

of the moon, gravity a curse they wrote
in sand near where nuns drank

homemade dandelion wine until their hearts
crawled out of their chests

and clicked songs they sang before they loved
and gave up on the world.

The heart's a glove that could catch the sky
and still have room

for an obstinate boy's desire for women
whose bodies are rumors

whispered under dark robes he believes
tremble with tattoos of dandelions

they touch naked at night saying the rosary,
their hearts full of sawdust and curses

carved on walls exact distances from anything
that could pass for love.

The crabs long for the clarity of words,
not vague signs. Nuns dream of

touching the boy whose baseball cap is
a feckless moon that confesses

to a beach where every grain of sand is
another name of a saint

a nun whispers, naked and dancing in
the ecstatic drift of dandelions

in the dark over a dirt-patched field
where, earlier, boys had

hurled the madness of a dull white ball
at one another as if to shatter

some stained-glass figure whose heart is
a moon that mumbles curses

and collapses in their chests when they touch
themselves thinking of

the tattooed bodies of nuns. The crabs form
a saint's name on the chapel walls,

and a boy locked in for the wrong words
reads the name and cries.

The heart is a nun with The Assumption
tattooed on her stomach

as though her flesh were stained glass.
Clouds of dandelions rise

with the Virgin. The sky burned on
the belly of this nun is enough

to consume the heart of any boy,
bring him to the chapel,

and make him lie down with crabs
who long for the moon as if it were

the only beach on which they could love.
He will touch the crosses

carved on their bodies and sing the names
of the saints he knows

are tattooed on his heart.
When he's done,

a nun will lead him out to the cloister
where she'll drift dandelions over him

before straddling his taut body
and miming the motions of the heart.

A woman with only one name was found on this road
by coyotes and a ghost singing of not coming back.

Later, after police have stammered over her,
you read her single-column story in the local paper

next to a quarter-page ad for a production of *Turandot*
and believe her body had pointed the way out.

You drink in the one bar in this bruised town and hum,
a dead woman's name on your lips, believing

music can reclaim anything, even the sad dust
on bottles of foreign cordials no one in this town

ever asks for. They've named the road after the woman.
Every local story ends with horseflies. And dust.

Or a ghost drunk in the bar where the only waitress
sings hymns so low no one can make out the words.

Her body is a fugue. The ghost believes his name
in her breath could save this town. These days

horseflies hum a dead woman's name. Coyotes come
down out of the mountains and roll around in trash

and howl. You want music to bring everything back,
and hum a waltz in your throat. The coyotes

start what could be a box step. You ask the waitress
to dance, her red hair the color of the earth

carved by a river the ghost fished in Italy. The two of you
waltz in front of the bar. The jukebox drones

a sad tune about gold and lust and the thick taste
of cordials. Dust flowers in the scratches. Ghosts,

it's been said, hear the blues in every woman's name.
Insects here hum requiems no one writes down.

Coyotes leave tracks that score what the ghost would
swear was an opera. The jukeboxes in this town

don't know Italian and so they can't play Puccini.
No one's drunk enough to bear the guilt that makes

hymns of his women. Even those with only one name.
You try to tell the waitress how he died in Brussels

with *Turandot*, unfinished, in his hands. Even if he had
finished the opera, no jukebox would play it.

The waitress doesn't care that Puccini often couldn't
make it home from the bar in Torre del Lago.

That he wrote *Who has lived for love has died for love*.
You give up and head home, knowing no opera

is more tragic than this sore town that names roads
for the bodies of dead women who knew

what Puccini knew. The point of flesh is love.

from Meditations Before the Windows Fail

To begin with, this sky
doesn't have a clue & can't be said
to clearly predict what's coming.

Filtered through clouds gray enough
to seem wise, this light says

art is a failed translation
of how the world is. A room

in a hotel in a landscape flat enough
wind never slows
enough to catch its breath,

the drapes shut, ignores
what's coming down outside

& lets lovers lie, worn out
& damp, on a bed out of whack
with its frame enough to be

said to be aslant, or askew.
That is, if someone other
than the lovers were to walk in,

cursing what was coming down
outside, & stop in mid-curse,

having come to the conclusion
it's not their room. The world is
off enough to allow for anything.

Distance always has the last word,
though. The lovers
always knew it was coming.

SOMETHING WHIMSICAL WITH LIGHT

Nothing funny about a sky like this.
Crows, though, could be

laughing, the joke private & on us.
Memory's at risk, light a blur

we'd have to say is indistinct
at best. A chuckle

might be possible, if a cloud
did something whimsical with light.

And in dim hotel rooms, lovers
laugh at the silly positions

they sometimes find themselves in, passion
a mystery often comic.

Ode in Someone Else's Voice

This sky reminds me how difficult it is
to praise anything that moves us

& not have that praise turn maudlin
or end up ravaged & broke in some alley,

the taste of emptiness in its mouth
as it mumbles hollow promises

& asks for a dollar to buy a Danish
& a cup of coffee. How we want

to look away & hurry past this
sorry reminder of what it means

to accept the inherent pleasures of this world
for what they are & not turn them into

something more *us* than *other*. We want
all praise to come back to us

& we'll sing someone else's lyrics
as if we had written them & don't care

how our voice changes them. To light
on a day like this, any subterfuge

seems silly & just not worth the effort.
I want to be able to sing, in the voice

of this light, of lovers, their tongues
writing odes on one another's flesh.

THE SKY MIGHT AS WELL BE A PRIEST

Last night the moon was a scythe
low in the sky & so beautiful

death, glimpsing itself in its orange blade,
smiled & took the night off.

This morning, the memory
of that blade of a moon
carves graffiti on my rough heart.

I want to swing the scythe that is memory
or the sliver of a moon

through the fields between here & Ohio
& cut down every weed

that grows despite the emptiness
in the language locals mumble

into a sky that might as well be a priest,
they confess so much to it.

There's nothing to keep me from
a hotel room & a woman
lovely enough to gather what's been cut

&, with it, weave together a man
who would shiver awake
in her arms, confess everything.

This sky has my number.
Not far off a siren wails,
the first Wednesday of the month.

This is a test, I know. That the sky has passed
the point of giving up
anything is a comfort, unexpected.

This light pretends the cold's a memory.
It isn't. And lovers aren't
picky about time, which is, after

all, an odd fellow who hums tunes
no one can sing the words to,

though everyone swears the song is
one they've sung along with
as it came out of jukeboxes & car radios.

No music someone has slipped quarters into
a slot to hear could be mistaken
by anyone for any kind of siren.

But it could be a warning to lovers
to hang on. That flesh is
the only redemption possible

in this world. That the tongues
of lovers have to tease
what meaning's possible from flesh.

TO HELL WITH THE DECONSTRUCTIONISTS

Nothing about this sky suggests how to read it.
To be critical of light made spurious

by clouds seems petty & too predictable,
& any birds are too far off to be named.

Once the sky brokered a deal with the devil
& called itself a deluge

a man & woman rode out in some hotel room,
writing texts on one another with their tongues.

To hell with the deconstructionists.
The body was what they tasted & nothing more.

The lovers would have said they didn't need
any explanation, any other text.

Luck isn't a concept this sky would stoop to
understand, or give in to. This wind,

brazen & all too sure of the inevitable,
whistles through fingers crossed as if an inane gesture
could determine the outcome of anything.

Crows sprawled in the branches of a dying oak
could be mistaken, from a distance,

for letters, shaky, as if the hand that scrawled them
had trembled from exposure
to cold & the memory of a hotel room

where fingers, warm, slipped into a lover's body
& the shivering that followed was enough

to make any sky an advertisement for gambling,
a billboard plastered with hands the size of condominiums
letting fly dice in search of numbers.

Nothing is so random as convincing
lovers holding one another

they have to let go, to give this up. Not even
the sky, with all its light, should
be able to do such a number on lovers.

Better they ignore the sky & its pale certainty.
Better they let passion determine the odds.

The sky let loose, all bets are off,
the game rigged, someone at a radar screen
pretending the edge of a front is

the curve of a woman's hip
he imagines tracing with his tongue

in some hotel room, curtains drawn
to forget what's coming down outside
where everything's released,

the world one long shiver, a low moan
of light coming from the one lamp post

close enough to the hotel room a woman,
shivering, might notice it
through where the curtains don't quite meet

& think it odd that this distant light
sings what sounds like a hymn

as she comes, the man's tongue
touching her to a music
that seems to match what she hears

the lamp post humming,
all one music the sky's let loose.

IN THE FORM OF AN OPERA BY MOZART

This white-out of snow is the rumor of an aria
in an unknown opera by Mozart.

The first scene opens on what seems to be
a hotel room, the curtains drawn, only one lamp on.
The room has the feel of expectation.

A solitary violin begins playing
what will be this opera's theme.

A man holds a woman as if she were memory.
They dance, not to the violin's quaint music

but to an orchestra out of the past
that lures the moon out of the sky to listen.

Later, the woman straddling the man in bed,
the wind instruments & the brass
have their various ways with the theme.

Their bodies follow the music's lead.
Outside, the world is missing.
The lovers collapse into one another.

After, the man takes the violin to his chin
& plays the theme from the opening scene,
the music that's been here all along.

from What Light Becomes: The Turner Variations

THE BEAUTY OF IT

after The Burning of the Houses of Lords and
Commons, *October 16, 1834*

Knowing it isn't just light, this burning
that from here, the other side of
the Thames, torches a compromised sky
as if it were an act of fierce revenge

nothing could justify, the beauty of it
seems, reflected in the sluggish river,
a longing for someone to notice
how this canvas stills such ferocity

and keeps it dynamic and reaching for
more air to detonate. How delicate
the hint of a bridge against the pure lack

of detail the conflagration's determined
to insist on, as if jealous. As if
to consume a world couldn't be enough.

In All the Best Ways

after Ainwick Castle, *c.1829*

It's the sort of moon that seems to argue
for the presence of ghosts. Deer lower
antlered heads as if in acknowledgement
of the dead stumbling stiff and confused

over grass that, alive, they had loved in,
wet and moaning. Dead, they find they have to
envy it. Deer, content to simply drink
moonlight from the shallow river, ignore

the man in one of the few lit windows
of this castle which has never been this
shade of blue. It could be he's dancing,

moving towards a woman who's warm and wet
in all the best ways. It could be the moon's
out for lovers, not the dead, after all.

IN GAUDY COSTUMES

after Sun Setting Over a Lake, *c.1840*

An indefinable number of ghosts
huddle, a murmuring of absent flesh
or its memory, in the sorrowful hint
of what once might've been a row boat

adrift in what passes for water
at times like this. Ghosts hum, in perfect sync,
old show tunes. One is so moved she leaps out
onto the fogged-over lake and starts in

on an elaborate waltz last witnessed
in some elegantly-gilded ballroom
filled with half-drunk Venetian men and women

in gaudy costumes who would head for home
in gondolas sculled through fog by humming
gondoliers who could've, themselves, been ghosts.

THINGS THE DEAD HAVE FORGOTTEN

after Venice: The Grand Canal, with Santa Maria della
Salute, from Near the Hotel Europa, *1840*

A distant storm has passed, or is
passing. Call it *intercession*, and don't
ask. The dead, rowing their stark gondolas,
cross wavering reflections of buildings

where the living do things the dead have
forgotten. So much water. The city
of Venice ever drowning, the air is
alive with more than the dead, with insects

too small and numerous to ever name
with certainty. Beauty's nothing more
than a particular moment, the light

turning the stark Baroque dome beneath
the storm bone-white so it seems to plead
for something like memory for the dead.

WHILE MAGICIANS SLEEP

after Venice: A Gondola in a Storm, *1840*

What's coming is indescribable,
this but another pathetic attempt
at description. Maybe we are
mistaken more than we care to admit.

So much of our time we watch one gathering
or another of what is, after all,
what we are, mostly, loving
how water vapor composes the sky

into operas. The facades of buildings
fade in light of this storm's furious advance.
Magicians sleep in rooms gone

or going translucent, chanting, in
their sleep, incantations meant to stop
the world from becoming nothing but light.

DARKER THAN ANY BLACK

after Peace—Burial at Sea, *1842*

What looks to be a stray light reflecting
off a sacred artifact of gold
sears the misted dark, and disparages
the sheer domination of those sails

Turner wanted the skill to make darker
than any black had ever been.
A teal balances the audacity
of the cold light of the flare shot off

in the distance with the authenticity
of its body. Something's gone out of
the world worth missing. The severing

of one dark into two isn't a prayer
for the dead but for the living, to
remind us memory's a sacrament.

DRUNK WITH LIGHT'S RETURN

after Norham Castle, Sunrise, *c.1845*

The skeletal stray bent to sip water
the most substantial thing for miles,
even *its* reflection dissolves
in the resolute madness of rumor

or innuendo. Chanted, vague echoes
fill castle rooms where walls tremble
with a ghostly music made drunk by
light's return, enough to inebriate us,

numbing our feet so our waltz with
the dawn isn't so much etiquette
as it is spiritual, a primal act.

It's enough to say the world is drunk
on mornings like this, everything hazy,
ephemeral, something we could inhale.

CLOSE ENOUGH

after Luxembourg: The Citadel of St-Esprit, with the
Louis and Beck Bastions, *c.1839*

Altitude doesn't equal perspective,
though it might make it easier to see
the slow approach of ruin. This spire
could be a road sign set in place

for The Rapture. If it doesn't rain,
those taken up might stop here, being
mistaken, thinking they're already home.
From here, all the screams and prayers

and sobbing wouldn't have far to go
to be heard clear to heaven. To be
close enough to the sky to find it

hard to breathe clarifies a language,
making rough-hewn letters, so huge as to be
invisible, visible. A prayer for here.

ALL SIENNA

after Venice: The Giudecca Canal, Looking Towards
Fusina at Sunset, *1840*

Only the dead can say how far the blue
distance is, the living more concerned
with how soon every bit of light might be
gone. Everything's reflected. The buildings

in the water, grainy and slightly more
vague. And the living, in their gondolas,
headed to Fusina, overwhelmed
by the spectacle that is and will be,

for a time, the sky, as well as the faint,
harried images, all sienna, of
the dead doing their grim version of rowing

into a distance only they can guess.
The dead, in Venice, laze in varied hues
of earth, reflecting the living, timeless.

WHAT COULD BE A PRAYER

after The Evening Star, *1829-30*

No horizon's ever been more of an ache.
What could be the ruined mast and spars
of a ship sunken in the shallows
jut from low tide as if to meliorate

any longing become musculature pain
this contentious and resolute marking
of what is sky and what's not leads to
if we look. The boy, his net full of shrimp,

refuses distinctions, despite his dog's
curious insistence. How it leaps at
the stark horizon and barks what could be

a prayer some sleeping magician mutters
to delay the onset of dusk and deny
anything as absolute as this horizon.

Some Ghostly Architecture

after Going to the Ball (San Martino), *1846*

It's not what's being celebrated,
but that being is celebrated. Venice
has a way of acknowledging the past
without anyone feeling it's in the way

of this stippled reflection of the sky
we row through, this second sky we tremble
with our passing through it. To set light
aquiver with just our hands in water

can make the heart, surrounded, as it is,
by what's essentially dirty water
in the chest, feel like a gondola adrift

in the rueful reflection of a sunset,
rowing toward some ghostly architecture
in the distance, a cordial music calling.

AN ELEGANT ARCHITECTURE

after The Church of Notre Dame and St Laurent, with
the Chateau of Lo51uis Philippe Beyond, *1845*

"He's quite mad, you know," the Queen's reported
to have said. Is it madness to see
with precision and passion, in balance?
If so, and if clarity can be said

to be possible with such vision,
if that which might be insubstantial
can, with his arrogance, be seen
as though it is the most *real* in fact,

cherish his madness. How light both defines
and dissolves the elegant architecture
of this church, making it more a psalm

than a structure. To see both stone and sky
as elusive steps in the waltz that is
light may be madness, but it leaves us *touched.*

WHAT LIGHT BECOMES

after Venetian Festival, *c.1845*

Luminosity, like any concept,
needs to be imagined to be said
to exist. As soon as anything
distinguishes itself enough to be

named, all hope's lost. When it comes to
luminosity, a giving over
to light, the most subtle brushstrokes
determine on canvas what light becomes,

and anything you're told to see slows down
your seeing. The crowds waiting to
witness once more the exact moment

light becomes color are no more alive
than the dead who scuttle around and leave
tracks luminous enough to lead us home.

The poems in this volume have appeared in the following books:
Animals Housed in the Pleasure of Flesh, Bluestem Press, 1995. *Attendant Ghosts,*
Cleveland State University Poetry Center, 2000. *The Precarious Rhetoric of Angels,*
White Pine Press, 2005. *Open Between Us,* Turning Point, 2010. *A Short Bestiary of
Love and Madness,* Stephen F. Austin State University Press, 2011. *Monks Beginning
to Waltz,* Truman State University Press, 2012. *Structures the Wind Sings Through,*
Full/Crescent Press, 2014. *Meditation Before the Windows Fail,* Lost Horse Press,
2015. *What Light Becomes: The Turner Variations,* Red Mountain Press, 2019.

The author would like to express his sincere and lasting gratitude to the following
people for their invaluable help as friends and readers and inspiration for the
poems in this collection: Douglas Smith, Mairi Meredith, Stephen Dunn, Andrea
Van Vorhis, Wayne Barham, Joanna Howard, Michael Karl Ritchie, James De
Crescentis, Misty Messenger Mulligan, Molly Priest, Larissa Szporluk, Paula
Lambert, Diane Walk, Ruth Ann McCray, Michael Czyzniejewski, Karen Craigo,
Tom Noyes, Aimee Pogson, Al Maginnes, Philip Terman, Greg Morris, Eugene
Cross, Wendell Mayo, and, of course, Susan Gardner and Red Mountain Press.

He would also like to acknowledge the support of the following organizations:
The Ohio Arts Council, The Pennsylvania Council on the Arts, The National
Endowment for the Arts, and Penn State Erie, The Behrend College.